DISCARD

GUDRUN

GUDRUN

Alma Johanna Koenig

TRANSLATED FROM THE GERMAN
BY ANTHEA BELL

LOTHROP, LEE & SHEPARD BOOKS
NEW YORK

English translation copyright © 1979 by Kestrel Books
First published in Great Britain in 1979 by Kestrel Books
All rights reserved. No part of this book may be reproduced or utilized in any form or by any means, electronic or mechanical, including photocopying, recording or by any information storage and retrieval system, without permission in writing from the Publisher. Inquiries should be addressed to Lothrop, Lee & Shepard Books, a division of William Morrow & Company, Inc., 105 Madison Ave., New York, N.Y. 10016.
Printed in the United States of America.
First U.S. Edition　1 2 3 4 5 6 7 8 9 10

Library of Congress Cataloging in Publication Data
Koenig, Alma Johanna, 1887?–1942?
Gudrun.
Translation of Gudrun.
SUMMARY: A prose retelling of the 13th-century epic poem that follows the fluctuating fortunes of Gudrun, daughter of a king, who spends many years as the hostage of the evil queen of Normandy.
1. Gudrun—Juvenile literature. [1. Gudrun. 2. Knights and knighthood. 3. Middle Ages] I. Title.
PZ8.1.K73Gu 1979　　　831'.2　　[398.2]　　79-917
ISBN 0-688-41899-6　　ISBN 0-688-51899-0 lib. bdg.

PEOPLE IN THE STORY

HAGEN, King of Ireland.
HILDE, his daughter (her name is pronounced just like its modern English version, "Hilda").
HILDBURG, daughter of the King of Portugal, Hilde's companion and friend.
HETTEL, King of the Hegelings, overlord of thirty countries along the North Sea coasts. Among his followers, the rulers of those countries, are:
HORAND of Denmark, a skillful minstrel;
FRUTE of Denmark, a wise old counselor;
WATE of Stürmen, a strong and fierce warrior, descended from the giants (his name, and Frute's, both have two syllables, the final 'e' being pronounced as it is in Hilde's name);

MORUNG of Frisia;
IROLD of Waleis.
GUDRUN, daughter of Hettel and Hilde.
ORTWIN, Gudrun's younger brother, King of Ortland.
THE PRINCE OF THE MOORS, one of Gudrun's suitors.
LUDWIG, King of Normandy.
GERLIND, Ludwig's wife.
HARTMUT, son of Ludwig and Gerlind, another of Gudrun's suitors.
ORTRUN, his sister.
HERWIG, King of Zealand, betrothed to Gudrun.
HILDBURG, daughter of Hildburg of Portugal and Morung, Gudrun's friend.
HEREGART, a duchess, one of Gudrun's companions.

GUDRUN

CHAPTER ONE

Hagen the Devil
How Horand sang the song of Fair Hilde
King Hettel sent his men to Ireland
How Lord Wate learned the three strokes
of the Irish swordsmen

In Ireland, very long ago, there lived a king called Hagen who was fierce and wild. When he was called Hagen the Devil, he only laughed. He was stronger than ordinary men, so tall that his dark head rose above the fair heads of his followers like a thorn bush above wheatfields.

The wandering minstrels said, in their songs, that Hagen was so fierce because a griffin bird had stolen him away when he was a child, and he had a hard time of it struggling to survive on the desert island where the griffin lived. And the minstrels said he had brought his beautiful queen back from the griffin's island. But that was all in the past, and now the Queen of Ireland had a daughter, a young girl even more beautiful than her own mother ever was. There was magic in young Hilde's face, and many great kings, once they had set eyes on her, sent their men to her father asking for her hand in marriage. But though their envoys might ride into the castle courtyard of Ballygan very grandly, with trumpets blowing, they all died miserably at the end of a rope.

Hagen the Devil had more than twenty such envoys hanged, sent the ropes home to their masters, and told them he would not give his child to anyone who was not a greater king than himself.

Meanwhile, the minstrels' song of the beauty of Hilde went swiftly from land to land, like a swallow flying in the spring, telling how she was a prisoner in her grim father's hands, just as her mother had been the griffin's prisoner. The song reached faraway Denmark, where Lord Horand lived. Horand was a vassal of King Hettel of the Hegelings; he was young, a good knight and a good fighter, and as a singer he had no equal in all the lands around.

Once he had heard the song of Fair Hilde, he could not get its sweet, simple tune out of his head.

He began dreaming of it, wove melodies around the

notes, he made the words more passionate, and when he sang the song in his own way by night, in his lonely fortress by the sea, the fishermen stopped pulling in their heavy nets to listen, and the fish they had caught escaped.

It so happened that King Hettel invited all the great men who were his vassals, owing him allegiance and paying him homage as their sovereign, to a feast. No king ever had such great knights to serve him as Hettel. Of all the great princes he invited the most famous was Lord Wate of Sturmen. People said he was descended from the ancient race of giants. Wate's beard hung down to his waist, and his hair flowed wildly around his shoulders. He seemed a kind, generous man, and when he laughed the whole room echoed to the sound, but in the fury of battle he spared nothing in his path, slaughtering babies in their cradles in case they grew up to avenge their fathers.

When all King Hettel's guests had feasted merrily, the king asked his friend Lord Horand to sing for them. However, when Horand picked up his harp he seemed unable to remember any of the beautiful songs that had made him so famous. Hard as he thought, the only tune he had in his head was the minstrels' song of Fair Hilde, and so he sang it in front of other people for the first time, out loud in the king's hall, with all the sweetness of his voice in every verse. When he had finished, they were all quiet for a long time.

Then King Hettel, lost in thought, said, "How happy the

man would be who married such a girl! Who is the woman in your song, Horand?"

"She is Hilde, daughter of the King of Ireland," the singer answered. The words seemed heavy on his tongue, as if some magic spell forced him to utter them.

King Hettel brought his fist down on the table. "Well, there's an end to something that never begun!" he said, and Horand breathed again.

But Lord Frute of Denmark, King Hettel's wise counselor, whose blue eyes saw further than other men's, said, "I have heard a great deal about Hilde of Ireland, and I have thought for some time that she would make a fine queen for the Hegelings. You should send men to ask for her hand in marriage, Lord Hettel!"

However, the king replied, reluctantly, "I know that Hagen the Devil hates everyone who wants to marry his daughter! Many good men have died trying to win her. Do you want me to send my own faithful followers for Hagen to hang?"

"Send Wate, Lord Hettel!" said Frute. "He is the best messenger anyone could have."

Wate leaped to his feet so violently that the table shook. "If that is your advice, you would not be sorry to see me dead!" he said. "I saw Hagen the Wild in his youth, when he killed the griffin single-handed, I have never seen such a man since, and I would not be very willing to pit myself against him! Still, if Lady Hilde is as beautiful as Horand sings, and if she is to be your wife, Lord Hettel, as Frute suggests, I will be your messenger. But I want Horand and Frute, who put the idea into your head, to go with me and suffer the same hardships!"

Hettel looked into his friend Horand's face. Bending toward him, he said softly, "Quick, Horand! Sing us another song, and let us all forget Hilde!"

Without glancing at the king, Horand said, "I know a man whose king saved his life in a battle against the Saracens; the king himself was so badly wounded he was near death for many days afterward. The man he had saved swore by his overlord's wounds that ever afterward Hettel's wishes should mean more to him than his own, and he would put Hettel's life before his own. That man's name, I think, was Horand." The singer raised his eyes to the king's, and spoke out loud. "It was decided I would be your envoy to Ireland from your first word and your first glance, before Frute gave you his advice."

When young Lord Morung of Frisia heard that he laughed cheerfully. "If Wate and Frute and Horand are going to Ireland, I will go on the adventure too!"

Then there was talking and argument, and in the end it turned out that none of the heroes wanted to stay behind. They promised to avenge the good men Hagen had killed, and show him the Hegelings were stronger than the Irish. Hettel's face was very troubled, but in the middle of all the noise Frute said to him, "You must give your country an heir, Lord Hettel, and I know of no girl of nobler blood than Hilde. But if you will listen to my advice, it may save Wate's life, and everyone else's too. . . . Have ships of cypress wood built, cover the masts with silver, fit them out with silken sails, and make them strong enough to hide a thousand armed men in their holds. And put jewels on board, and good weapons, and the kind of things that women like. My nephew Horand shall act as captain of a fleet of peaceful merchants!"

Horand took a deep breath, and then said, laughing, "Who minds a long voyage when there are pretty girls to be seen at journey's end? I will do it!"

The other men all laughed too, and they sat talking over Frute's stratagem. He said only a few of the very best men should be seen up on deck, while all the others stayed hidden down below.

Wate was the only one to hesitate. "I shall be a poor hand at acting the merchant! All my life I have given gifts freely to my friends, without asking for anything in exchange! I would rather fight the Irish than trade with them!"

Hettel and Frute talked for a long time, and they made their plan that night, down to the last detail. They decided the adventurers would set out at the beginning of May, to give themselves time to prepare the ships and provisions, weapons and merchandise they would need.

Soon King Hettel sent his lords home to their own countries, with great goodwill, telling them not to trouble about horses or clothes because he would equip them and all their followers so well that every man there would be fit to come into the company of beautiful women.

So when May came, troops of men rode to King Hettel's court along roads that were wet with spring showers.

Hettel had promised them rich armor, but the princes all prided themselves on arming and clothing their own men as magnificently as themselves. It was not until they took their horses and shields on board, however, that they saw what rich cargoes the ships were carrying. The Hegelings embarked, and every one of the men who were to stay in hiding down below swore Frute a solemn oath that nothing at all—no sense of curiosity, no kind of discomfort—would tempt him to come up on deck before Frute gave the word.

Hettel himself rode down to the seashore. His face was pale and troubled. Saying goodbye to Horand, he embraced him and whispered in his ear, "My heart is heavy, and I could almost wish you had never sung me that song of Fair Hilde!"

The Hegelings set sail, with a fair north wind behind them. For twenty-six days they saw nothing but the sky above them, blue as a field of flax in flower, and the blue sea below.

And every night Horand sat in the bows, his legs over the ship's side, and sang to the glittering stars. One man who heard him used to swear, to his dying day, that he saw the mermaids come up out of the sea to listen nightly, their fishtails all swaying in the glassy green water.

On the twenty-seventh morning they saw the coast of Ireland ahead, and Frute took the tiller, warning them to beware of rocks. For the closer they came, the more rugged did the coastline look, with long outcrops of rock eaten into by the tides, red rock such as the Hegelings had never seen before, washed by the constant movement of the waves. Sometimes the rocks rose up like the vaulted gateway of some unseen fairy castle, sometimes they were strangely shaped, like stony sentries larger than mortal men.

"I do not like the look of those rocks," said young Lord Irold of Waleis, running his hand through his brown hair. "They are red, red as blood: a bad omen!"

Horand laughed at him. "I can see a better omen there than you! These red rocks reflect the fire we shall light for the wedding feast!"

They made slow progress, expecting an enemy attack at any moment, but they met nothing but gulls and sea swallows swooping through the air. Then, when the coastline became gentler, falling smoothly down to the sea, they saw huge flocks of sheep, white as clouds. Old shepherds, clothed in sheepskins themselves, raised wrinkled hands to shield their eyes and peered suspiciously at the foreign ships sailing by. Darkness came, and Frute advised them to keep away from the shore and cast anchor well out to sea. But when they came ashore in the morning to get drinking water, they saw river valleys among green hills, valleys lonelier and more beautiful than they had ever dreamed of.

On the thirty-sixth day Lord Morung waved to his companions from the mast, shouting. Interrupted in their meal, the men on deck flung down their beakers and ship's biscuit, jumped up and ran to look. They saw such a sight as they had never seen before.

Stone by stone, as far as the eye could see, a great causeway made of basalt stones stretched out before them. It was built for steps larger than those of human beings: the last remains of an ancient dancing floor from the days when the giants' sons ruled the land. It had stood for centuries and you can see it in Ireland to this very day.

Wate nodded his head. "I knew that Hagen the Devil and I had ancestors in common! Why, the hilt of my sword grew hot in my hand at the sight of this place!"

They crossed the giants' ancient bay silently, armed and ready. Granite cliffs, steep as sheer walls, fell to the rough sea. There were no trees or grass on them; they were like ramparts shielding the gods themselves from human sight. The cry of eagles rang in the Hegelings' ears, and the sound of the wind, and the rush and roar of waterfalls. Horand felt it was only now he truly understood the songs about Hagen's wild nature and Hilde's beauty, for Ireland itself seemed to him both beautiful and wild.

At last they sighted Hagen's castle of Ballygan, perched like an eagle's eyrie among black rocks. It was built of unhewn blocks of the same black stone; they were wedged together to form round arched gateways, they were piled up to build the high walls; there were narrow windows up at the very top, a giddy height above the ground, and a round, flat-roofed tower. Birds of prey hovered, screeching, above the heads of the sentries on that tower, who had sighted the ships by now. They were so high up that the sound of their horns blowing was only a faint echo in the Hegelings' ears.

They sailed around the spur of the mountain, and it was just as Frute had said: ahead of them lay a great harbor full of ships, mast beside mast. The place was swarming with people who came up to welcome and question the Hegelings. The Irish were well-dressed and well-spoken, and the Hegelings thought Ireland must be a fine place to live.

They reefed in their white silk sails and began to carry their goods ashore: great barrels and crates and bales of everything the heart could desire. The Irish, who had never seen such rich merchants in such splendid ships before, came hurrying up from all sides. There stood sixty princes who had taken King Hettel for their overlord and made this voyage for his sake, crying their wares, and smiling courteously to the people. Frute and Horand, wearing the richest clothes of all, acted as the two chief merchants.

Messengers ran to tell Hagen of this strange event, and he commanded his men to ride down to the shore with him. A path wound gently down the hillside of Ballygan, and soon the Hegelings saw Hagen the Devil riding down it on his black stallion, the only horse strong enough to bear his weight. The Hegeling heroes went to meet him and exchange greetings, and Hagen's eyes, under their bushy brows, rested on Wate in amazement. The king asked the strangers' names and where they came from, which was his right as host. Then wise old Frute let his head sink on his breast, and sighed deeply.

"We are poor merchants from far away, and we have suffered great unhappiness. Allow us to offer our goods for sale, my lord, and let us shelter here!" As Frute spoke, Lord Wate stood behind him, wearing a mailshirt secretly under his robes, like all the Hegelings, his hand gripped the hilt of his sword, ready to strike.

But King Hagen was not a man to grudge hospitality to strangers who approached him with courtesy. He assured his guests they would be left in peace and might come up to the castle, and he threatened to punish anyone who tried to make off with the strangers' goods.

Reluctantly, Wate let go the hilt of his sword.

Frute offered the king a gift of precious goblets made of good, heavy gold, worth a thousand marks. And he gave all Hagen's men shields and necklets; the Irish were amazed at the magnificence of the presents. Then Frute asked whether they themselves might bring gifts fit for noble ladies up to the castle. The strange merchants led twelve Arab horses on land; their coats were white as birch bark and their nostrils rosy as the heels of a year-old child. Their necks were arched like swans' necks as they pressed their muzzles to their chests, flakes of foam flying from their nostrils, while they pranced on gently hobbled feet, restless after the long sea voyage.

Frute also had twelve knights' shields brought to shore, heaped up with circlets of fine gold for women to wear around their foreheads, and clasps to fasten cloaks, belt buckles, bracelets, all made of bright gold and set with jewels.

They carried on land a hundred bales of wonderful cloth, silk shot with gold, and brocade of a true crimson dye only to be found in Baghdad, and bales of the finest linen, whiter than cherry blossom.

Twenty-four knights, led by Horand and Irold, rode up to the castle with these gifts, all dressed like rich princes going to a king's court to be made knights.

As they approached, Hagen's chief chamberlain exclaimed, "Why, I would set the value of those gifts at twenty thousand marks!"

Hearing that, Hagen gave orders for the gifts to be shared out among all the women of his court, and double their worth to be given to the merchants. He made Horand and Irold sit beside his own high seat, and asked where they came from.

"We are homeless men, sir," said Horand, "who have come to Ireland to ask your favor. We offended a great king."

"Who is this king who has made you leave your castles and your own countries?" asked Hagen the Wild. "Looking at you, I should call the man a fool! He would have done better to keep you in his service!"

"His name is King Hettel of the Hegelings," said Horand. "He is very powerful, and has done great deeds. Our country is very beautiful, and I am afraid we can never be happy away from it."

"Well, I will make good all that Hettel has done to you," said Hagen, "and if you will stay here at my court, I will repay what your king took."

Horand thanked Hagen, as courtesy demanded, though he began to feel that Frute's trick was almost too clever; he found it hard to go on with it, when Hagen was treating them so kindly.

Hagen said he would have fine rooms made ready for

the Hegelings, and he offered them food and drink. But Frute, down by the ships, did not intend to eat with a man whom he meant to deceive, and he refused the offer, sending a message back to say, "We have plenty to satisfy us, even if we were used to eating nothing but gold and silver!"

The Irishmen who had brought Hagen's offer of hospitality down to Frute watched while he had the coverings taken off his cargo, and they thought they had never seen such magnificence before.

Nor were merchants ever known to sell their goods so cheaply; anyone who wanted could buy. If a poor man stood watching, at a distance, twisting his shabby cap, or a wide-eyed child loitered near, sucking its thumb, the Hegelings, smiling, would make the poor man or the child a present of what they could not afford to buy, and Horand stroked the children's flaxen heads.

However, all the time this cheerful trading went on, the rest of Hettel's men were lying hidden in the holds of the ships, wishing they could be up and fighting, not battened down here, idly drinking and playing dice.

Every day Hagen's chamberlains came back from the shore with marvelous tales of mothers to whom Frute had given fine linen for their newborn babies, debtors whose debts Wate had paid, hungry folk fed daily by Horand.

Fair Hilde had seen one of the Hegelings, only once, from her window, and she thought he was a finer man than any of the Irish lords she knew. She was so full of curiosity to see the other strangers too that she asked her father to invite his guests to court and thank them for their rich gifts. She had heard there was a giant among them, she said, and she would like to see this giant.

Hagen the Devil invited the Hegelings to his court, and on Frute's advice they accepted the invitation.

When the heroes came into the king's hall, Hagen himself went to meet them, as a sign of honor, and his queen rose and welcomed them with all her heart. However, not one of the Hegelings could tear his eyes from Fair Hilde. It was like a magic spell: she was so lovely that a warm sense of happiness overwhelmed anyone who so much as looked at her.

As for Hilde herself, she stood there quite unaware of it, but she felt afraid of Wate. She was glad he was no relative of hers, so she did not have to kiss him! He was so tall, and he had such a huge beard, though he had woven gold braid into it in honor of the occasion. Her hand lay in his like a little white mouse, and she could not help looking down to see if the mouse would escape unharmed. So she never noticed the tears come to Horand's eyes. He thought she was even sweeter than his dream.

When the women had left the hall, the men began to play board games. Some of the Irish went out into the courtyard, to compete with each other at throwing stones and spears and in swordplay.

Wate stood watching them, his arms crossed.

"Are you Hegelings as good at swordplay in your country as we Irish are in ours?" asked King Hagen.

"Why, no," said Wate, straight-faced. "I never saw swordfighting like this before! I'd be happy to spend a year learning the art, if one of your men would only teach me!"

"Then my very best swordsman shall be your teacher!" cried Hagen. "You may at least learn the three strokes of the Irish swordsmen; you will find them very useful in battle."

The swordsman came, and crossed blades with Wate, who was acting so clumsily that the Irish could hardly hide their laughter.

"Fetch my own sword!" cried Hagen. "I will teach Wate those three strokes myself!"

Pretending to be afraid, Wate said, "Oh, but promise not to wound me badly, sir!" Laughing, Lord Hagen promised.

However, once they began to fight and Wate felt how strong Hagen was, he forgot to play his part and fought in good earnest, thrusting so hard that Hagen's armor began to smoke under his blows, like a piece of wet wood in the fire.

"Well, now I have learned the three strokes of the Irish

swordsmen," laughed Wate, "so you need not spare me any longer!"

And they began a fight, exchanging thrust for thrust, that made the walls reecho. Neither Wate nor Hagen had ever fought such a strong opponent before.

They fought on and on, until the jasper pommels of both their swords broke off from the blades at the same moment. Then they went back to their seats. Hagen wiped the sweat from his brow.

"I never saw a pupil learn so fast before!" said he. "If I had known what fine swordsmen King Hettel's men were, I would not have taken my own sword down from the wall!"

CHAPTER TWO

*How Lord Horand sang the Saracen woman's song
How Hilde was carried off
King Hagen catches up with the Hegelings at Waleis
The battle on the shore
The heroes are reconciled
Hagen the Wild sees his daughter crowned
queen of thirty countries*

It had been a warm evening, and the night was mild. A gentle breeze carried the scent of thyme from the wide Irish sheep pastures. None of the Irish or the Hegelings had gone to bed. Now and then a sword clinked in the darkness, for the hall and courtyard were full of men, talking slowly in low voices, or putting back their heads to look at the wide, starry sky. Somewhere a nightingale was singing as if its little heart would break. Then Lord Horand began to play his harp.

When he struck the first chord, all the talking stopped. When he struck the second chord, all who had been lost in thought turned their heads to him.

When he struck the third chord, he began to sing, and as he sang the little nightingale itself fell silent.

There was magic on his lips. The tip of the ash tree in the castle courtyard stopped moving in the wind, and its leaves hung motionless in the moonlight as if turned to silver. The fountain stopped flowing, the cat that one of the Hegelings had been stroking stopped its purring.

Horand sang a song of a man who has seen his fate, and his fate is as fair as the only girl in the world he loves. His fate is to suffer longing, and the longing is his grave, for he will never win her. . . . Horand's song came to an end.

Suddenly the night was chilly with falling dew, and a wind sprang up. The fountain ran again, spraying a cold shower of drops; the cat gave the man's hand a fiery red scratch, he flung the animal away from him and it growled ferociously.

Horand the Dane wrapped his cloak around him, and walked away. At that moment a white glimmer, like the nightgown of a woman listening, disappeared from the upper window. But Fair Hilde could not sleep that night. She lay straining her ears, in case the fair-haired Dane would sing again, and whenever the nightingale struck up once more her heart stood still—she thought now he would sing too. But Horand did not sing again that night, nor the next night, nor the next. The heart of the king's daughter grew heavy, she went about in a dream, thinking of nothing but Horand's song. It was in her ears and on her lips, yet she could not quite sing it herself, nor could any of the Irish minstrels she asked.

One of Hilde's women was her dearest friend Hildburg, the lovely daughter of the King of Portugal. She saw Hilde's trouble sooner than any of the other girls, and secretly they discussed how they could get Horand to sing again.

One day, when King Hagen was sitting with his much-loved daughter, she plucked up courage to ask him, stroking his cheek timidly, "Dearest father, will you ask Horand to sing again, for me?" However, Hagen saw the way her eyelids fluttered, and heard her breath come short, and he felt the terrible rage that could overwhelm him rise within him.

"What, beg a wandering minstrel from a foreign land to approach my daughter?" he shouted, slamming the door behind him so hard that everything in the room shook.

Fair Hilde felt she would die if she could not hear

Horand sing again. She was in such despair and she cried so bitterly that her grief went to Hildburg's heart. Hildburg sent a faithful chamberlain to Horand asking him to come and sing for Hilde by night.

So when night came, the chamberlain led Horand along secret passageways to the hall where a single torch was burning. The king's daughter sat there, half hidden in the shadows, because she was afraid of her father's anger, with Hildburg kneeling beside her.

Horand bowed to them in silence. Then he began to play his harp, softly, very softly, and all the sleepers in the castle stretched and smiled in their dreams.

He began to sing in a low voice, like a mother singing her child to sleep, and all the time he never took his eyes from Hilde's face. She sat there motionless, eyes wide open and lips parted as she listened.

He sang a song of Amilé that he had learned from a Saracen woman one hot night, and it had never been sung before by any Christian man.

And as he sang, a rosebud standing in a vase burst into flower. As he sang, a shy deer came out of the forest with her fawn beside her, a fawn with a speckled coat as if the dappled sunlight were caught in it. The fawn came closer and closer on its shaky legs, and the two deer stood there in the full moonlight, heads bent to listen. Then Horand ended his song, and for a long time there was no sound at all in the hall where that one torch burned.

Fair Hilde slowly took a ring with a precious stone in it from her finger, and offered it to Lord Horand.

Horand of Denmark fell on one knee, and in the dim light his face seemed white as death.

"This ring is too great a gift for you to give me, princess! I know a better man; I am only his messenger. But if I might give him your ring, I know it would gladden his heart!"

"Who is this man?" asked Hilde. "A man who has someone like you to serve him?"

Rising from his knee and leaning on his sword—the sword on which he had sworn allegiance to the king—Horand spoke Hettel's name.

"When we left our homes, lady, we came of our own free will on behalf of our king, and we were not really outlawed. My king, Hettel, sends you his greetings, and you would be queen of thirty strong kingdoms if you would marry him!"

Out of the darkness, Hilde's faltering voice asked, "Is Lord Hettel a man like you, Horand?"

"He is a thousand times better than I am."

"Does Lord Hettel look like you, Horand?"

"He is taller and stronger than I am."

"Can Lord Hettel sing like you, Horand?"

"No, lady—for he has not paid the price for it, as I have." And at that moment the torch went out.

Just for a minute Horand thought there were tears in

Fair Hilde's voice as she said, "If you will swear me an oath to come and sing to me whenever I want, then I will be Hettel's wife."

And Lord Horand swore the oath.

When Frute saw Hilde's ring, he felt that his plan was working. He told Lord Irold to go to King Hagen and ask permission for them all to go. Irold, who was longing for his home and his young wife, found it quite easy to appear as happy as Frute had told him to seem at the prospect. He said that a message from King Hettel had arrived: the King of the Hegelings was not offended with his men any longer and he wanted them to come back.

Hagen was sorry when he heard that the Hegelings wanted to leave. He would have liked to keep Wate, above all, in his service, ever since he himself had felt the strength of Wate's sword.

He offered the Hegelings rich farewell gifts, but Frute refused them, making smooth speeches, and they did not take so much as a bracelet by way of a present. Instead, Frute asked Hagen to do them a favor before they left. Would he honor them by visiting their ships, along with his retinue and the noble ladies of his court, to see how the Hegeling seamen sailed?

When Hagen the Wild had granted this request, Frute had the heavy casks of wine, the tubs of salt meat and dried fish and bacon taken on land, and he fed all the poor people who came down to the shore. He knew that they would need to travel fast and carry very little cargo on their way home. So the Hegelings stood there giving away bales of warm cloth for nothing but a word of thanks—it was the cheapest trading ever seen.

Once the third day dawned, they would not let anyone come near the ships because King Hagen and the queen and princess were to be their guests.

At midday a loud cry rang out from the mast where Lord Morung, who had eyes a hawk, was keeping watch. The Irish were riding down in a long procession, a thousand men or more behind the king. And after the shining metal of their armor came the glowing colors of the ladies' robes as they too rode down.

The Hegelings welcomed their guests with great respect. But Frute had prudently divided up the rest of the cargo so that some of the ships held only weapons and men's gear, while others held the kind of merchandise that women like. So the Irish men were separated from the women on land, on board ship, and on the narrow gangplanks before they realized it.

One of them unhooked his own swordbelt so as to try out a Hegeling sword; another took off his armor to put on an Arabian mailshirt. Some of the men leaned their spears up in corners so that they could grasp pitchers of wine with both hands.

As for the women, they clustered around unrolled

bales of cloth and Arabian silks; they looked as if they were wading knee-deep in a gold and crimson sea. They laughed, and preened in front of mirrors, and even Hildburg did not notice how pale Fair Hilde was, or how hard she was breathing.

But in the middle of all this noise and laughter a sound rang out so loud that it seemed it would burst the ships' sides: Wate, blowing his great warhorn.

At that, trapdoors on the ships' decks fell in and up came the Hegelings who had been biding their time so many weeks down in the holds, shouting for joy.

The treasures were flung aside, no one cared where. Women's voices rose high and shrill, like gulls screaming, there was weeping, and the voices of men cursing as they searched for their swords, and the clash of weapons, and again and again came the echoing call of Wate's horn.

Up came the sails with a clatter, and a fair wind filled them. There was a great deal of splashing, for the Hegelings did not need to use their swords much; they simply threw the Irish into the sea one by one, as they rushed at them in confusion.

Hagen, however, seized the nearest boathook and struck down anyone in his way as he made for the ship where Hilde was standing. But the Hegelings drew up their gangplanks, giving any of the Irish who were fighting there a second baptism, and Hagen the Devil was among them; all his strength could not save him from a ducking in the sea. Anchors were hauled in, oars shot out, and Lord Morung, shouting with triumph, unfurled Hettel's white standard at the masthead.

Fair Hilde stood among her weeping women, upright and motionless. She was white as a sheet, and she had her hands over her ears to keep out the sound of her mother's cries.

Hagen the Wild was in a frenzy of rage. He himself helped push out the Irish ships into the sea, with all his furious strength. But they had been lying up all winter and were still leaky. The water came in through the cracks between the boards at once, and Hagen could tell it was impossible to put out to sea.

He sent for every shipbuilder in the country, threatening and bribing them to work from morning till night for seven long days, while he himself urged them to work faster, raging with impatience and helpless as a man in chains.

When the worst of the damage had been repaired, Hagen was the first man to leap on board. Three thousand of the Irish pursued the Hegelings with all sail hoisted, bailing out water with their helmets as they went.

Ever since his envoys had left, King Hettel had kept sentries posted along the coast, so that he would get news at once when they returned. But month after month went by, and Hettel's heart was heavy with grief when he thought of his friends.

One night, however, as he lay asleep, a chamberlain came to wake him. Hettel saw a messenger kneeling by his bed, gasping for breath. Yes, said the messenger, he himself had sighted the ships at Waleis, and all the heroes were on board, bringing a beautiful girl with them, the most beautiful girl he had ever seen in all his life.

Lord Hettel laughed. "The end of all our sorrow! Are you sure you are not deceiving me, my good man? Are you sure you're not lying when you say the girl was with them?"

"My lord," said the messenger, "I saw her as plain as I see you now! And I heard her say, in a little voice like this, 'Lord Horand, I am so afraid my father may catch up with us yet.'"

Lord Hettel laughed heartily at the messenger's imitation of a woman's voice and he gave him a hundred marks in gold and roused his men, in the midlde of the night, to ride to meet the lady.

Pages went scurrying along the corridors with torches, and the king's white castle of Matalane streamed with light. King Hettel himself was soon ready, sitting on his snorting stallion, and fast as his men tried to hurry, he thought it a long time before they could ride away from the court.

The sun was high in the sky when the Hegelings saw Hettel's banners waving. Horand straightened in his saddle.

"Now you will see Lord Hettel, lady!" he said, and Fair Hilde raised her timid eyes to his.

As for Lord Horand's face, it might have been carved from stone. He jumped down from his horse, threw the end of his cloak over his outstretched right hand, took Lady Hilde's own hand and led her forward; this was the custom of the Hegelings.

Fair Hilde saw one man ride out toward her, ahead of all the others. He dismounted and came striding forward.

"Is that King Hettel?" asked Lady Hilde, afraid, but Lord Horand did not answer. He greeted his king.

Lord Hettel's face was not like the face of the Danish lord which Hilde now knew so well, and he seemed many years older than Horand the singer. His smooth hair was interwoven with braid, his weapons were magnificent, the stuff of his cloak was rich, and yet Hettel himself was not quite how a young girl might imagine a great king for her lover.

Horand looked straight into his overlord's face, saying, "So I fulfill my promise to you, Lord Hettel!"

Slowly, he withdrew his hand from under Hilde's.

Then Hettel took her hand in a warm, firm grasp, and she heard his kindly voice saying, "I will always honor you, my queen, and you shall never have any reason to regret this day!"

She was in his arms, enclosed by the folds of his cloak, safely held as she had never been held before; and so Hilde received Hettel's first kiss.

Hettel and Hilde were married there in Waleis, the men were camped, while Frute's sentries kept watch to see if Hagen's fleet was coming yet. And Hilde's dearest friend, dark-haired Hildburg from Portugal, was married to Lord Morung of Frisia.

That night Lord Horand sang a new song, sweeter and sadder than any song he had ever sung before.

They say that one of Frute's sentries saw the forest spirit who was released from her spell by Horand's song. The story went that when the first white-robed Christian monks came to Waleis, a cruel princess tied one of them to a tree and shot arrows into him, laughing aloud at his torments. Then the monk cursed her, dooming her to wander in the forest forever, until she could weep for someone else's pain. When she heard Horand's song, it wrenched the tears from her breast like stones, and she wept for the first time in countless years. She went up to the singer and thanked him.

"I will reward you!" she said. "You shall have all the wealth a man could desire!"

"Very well!" smiled Lord Horand. "The poor and sick will be glad I have so much more to give them!"

"I see you do not want the same things as other men . . . so I will give you fame; fame as widespread as the blue chicory that flowers by every wayside. No one will sing any songs but yours."

"That would be a pity!" smiled Lord Horand. "What will the poor wandering minstrels do, if no one wants to hear their tunes any more?"

"Does fame not tempt you either?" asked the forest spirit, amazed. "Then let me lay my hand on your heart, and take away your pain forever!"

At that Horand leaped backward, both hands before his heart as if to protect it. "Do you want to return evil for good, and take away the only thing I have?"

Then the forest spirit walked quietly away from the singer, and as she went little white flowers sprang up where her hot tears fell.

In the morning, sea birds were screeching as they circled the cliffs, alarmed by the approach of the great Irish ships. And Horand the Dane, eyes burning after a sleepless night, saw Hagen's coat of arms on the red sails.

Sentry after sentry blew his horn; the call to arms echoed all along the steep coast. Wate quickly led the Irish women to the best ship, and put them in Morung's care. He told Morung to steer well out to sea, so that the poor women need not see too much of the fighting.

"What will become of us?" cried Lady Hilde. "Whoever lives or dies, we shall be unhappy now!"

The battle was beginning on the beach: Hagen the Wild was upon them. He did not even wait for his ship to drop anchor, but leaped overboard and began wading ashore, a great spear shaft in his hand. Lances shot past him like lightning, and his battle cry was so loud that Hilde could hear it. The young queen wept; she was afraid to see what was going to happen, and she knelt and prayed out loud for the lives of them all. So did Hildburg and all the other women, their terrified voices rising like a chorus.

Hagen had nursed his thoughts of revenge for many days, and now he hoped to cool his wrath. He cut himself a way through the Hegelings with his sword, and when he seemed to be going too slowly, he laid about him with the spear shaft. But King Hettel was calm and confident in war as well as peace. He made his own way slowly to Hagen and stood before him in all his power. Hagen struck his unknown son-in-law hard over the helmet. Hilde cried out, begging Lord Morung to go and protect Hettel, rather than herself. She was trembling at the sight of her father's anger, just as she had done ever since she was a child. By now, however, Wate's shield was above his master's head, ready to take the force of Hagen's next blow with the spear shaft. The shaft broke when it met that shield. Hagen and Wate, evenly matched in strength, fought each other without mercy. The battle died around them as everyone came up to watch warriors fight as they had never seen men fight before. But as Lord Hettel stood aside, bandaging his head, he heard Hilde's faint cry, and at once asked what she wanted. Then she begged him in tears, by her new-found womanhood, to end the fighting that would bring her so much sorrow. So King Hettel climbed on a tall rock and called out, "Hagen! Hagen!"

Hagen cried angrily, blood running down from a wound on his forehead into his mushy brows so that he could hardly see, "Who is that calling out and trying to part enemies?"

"It is Hettel of the Hegelings, and your daughter is queen of my thirty kingdoms."

Then Hagen said, less fiercely, "If you are Lord Hettel, you are not by any means the worst man I have met in battle. A warrior who can fight like Wate here would never serve a bad king!"

Hettel came up, his hand stretched out, and Hagen laid his own mighty right hand in it. Hettel took off his helmet and shouted over the battlefield that it was peace.

Hilde thought she had never heard sweeter words, though she could see how many men were hurt and how badly her father was wounded. Plucking up all her courage, she made Lord Morung steer the ship to shore. She climbed out and went over to Wate. For Horand had told her that as well as inheriting his immense strength from the giants, Wate had the ancient giantesses' knowledge of healing herbs. She begged him, hands clasped, not to forget her father and other wounded Irish warriors.

Wate, however, was loyal as a sheepdog who protects every new lamb in his master's flock as if it were his master himself. "I will not attend to Lord Hagen until he forgives you, my lady," he said. Hilde lowered her eyes, saying sadly, "My father cannot wish to speak to me, since he does not even ask to see me."

Wate went over to where the kings were sitting, the blood still trickling down Hagen's cheek from the bandage around his forehead.

"Your fair daughter, who is my queen, would like to tend your wounds, my lord, if she could be sure you would be glad to see her!"

Hagen the Wild had thought and thought about his child in the long nights, and he had found out that he could not conquer everything that stood in his path by sheer force. His face softened, and he said, "How could I not be glad to see my dear daughter in a foreign land?"

Then Horand the Dane took Lady Hilde's hand, and he and Frute led her to the kings. When Hagen saw her and Hildburg coming, he jumped up and welcomed her joyfully, trying not to let her see his wounds, cradling her against his broad breast and asking if she was happy here, and if she felt at home. Then Lady

Hilde raised her eyes to his, and told him frankly that she could never have chosen a better or nobler husband than Hettel.

Wate told the ladies to go aside, and he took the bandage off the sword cut he had made himself. He put an ointment on it, and some fresh herbs, muttering charms softly, and the blood stopped flowing as the wounds closed.

The warriors thought the battlefield was no place for women, and King Hettel invited Hagen and all his men to his castle of Matalane. By the time the heroes got there all the wounds Wate had treated were healed, leaving no scars at all behind.

As they rode through Waleis and the rest of the Hegelings' lands, Hagen saw rich farms and fields bearing a heavy harvest everywhere. Then he saw the white castle of Matalane rising up beside the sea: the most beautiful castle he had ever seen, made of well-hewn stones, with ramparts around it, and great arched windows, tall towers, and green ivy twining up its strong defensive walls. He saw his daughter crowned with the crown of the Hegelings and the crowns of twenty-nine other kingdoms, and he told her to be such a good queen that he and her dear mother need never feel ashamed when they heard news of her. He kissed Hildburg too, asking her to be a faithful friend to Hilde. Then Hagen told Hettel it was time for him to leave, since the oath he had sworn to give his child only to a greater king than himself had been fulfilled. Hagen and Wate were firm friends by now, and Hagen left Matalane with great rejoicing, praising Christ the Lord that everything had turned out so well.

It was a long time, however, before Queen Hilde summoned Horand to court to sing to her: not until her daughter, whom she called Gudrun, was born. Then Lord Horand came and knelt beside the cradle and sang —not loud, but softly, like whitethroats, warbling in their nests. He sang for a long time, his steadfast eyes fixed on the child, and she did not cry or move. They say Horand cast three magic spells around that cradle, to bring the baby three gifts: beauty to make brave men kneel; constancy, to be praised by minstrels in their songs; and grief—the grief the gods give to those they love . . .

CHAPTER THREE

Gudrun and her three suitors
How Hartmut of Normandy came himself
to try and win her
How she was betrothed to Herwig of Zealand

King Hettel ruled peacefully, with great honor, loving his queen dearly. By the time Queen Hilde had another child, a son and heir whom they called Ortwin, little Gudrun was running around the castle laughing her clear laughter.

When Ortwin was born his father gave him the kingdom of Ortland for his own, and as soon as he was old enough Lord Wate put him up before him on his own dapple-gray horse, and taught his tiny fingers how to hold a sword. Wate instructed him in the art of fighting. As for Gudrun, though she was still a child she grew lovelier every day. She spent some time at Lord Horand's home in Denmark, and he taught her many things that girls did not usually learn: knowledge of the world around her and the people in it, and he taught her to play the harp. He saw Gudrun growing up to be just as he had wished at her birth.

Her hair was golden; it hung down in two long, thick plaits which were interwoven with gold braid, but her hair itself outshone the braid. Her eyes were golden as young sea eagles, and her throat white as cherry blossom in springtime.

When she passed by, men would suddenly drop whatever they were holding, and then bend to pick it up, red in the face, staring after her and smiling incredulously. Women would sigh, and look puzzled, wondering exactly what it was which made that face so different, when it had eyes, a nose and a mouth just as theirs did.

One day the Prince of the Moors came on a long voyage to Matalane. His face was brown as the skins of forest deer, and he was a strong, handsome man. When he and his retinue visited King Hettel's court there was a tournament. Young Gudrun begged her mother so hard to let her watch that Lady Hilde agreed, and so Gudrun saw her first tournament, watching the foreign riders on their magnificent horses in amazement. They had leopard skins instead of saddles, and wore great gold rings in their ears.

When the Prince of the Moors heard her clear laugh, he glanced up, and his sword hand dropped. He thought he had never seen such a wonderful golden girl as Gudrun. That evening he asked King Hettel for her hand. But like many fathers, Hettel did not realize his daughter was a grown woman now; why, it seemed only yesterday he was listening to her first childish attempts to talk! He roared with laughter, as if the Prince of the Moors were joking. The Prince's brown cheeks grew red with anger, and he drove his dagger into the table in front of Hettel. The Arabian blade stuck there, quivering.

That very evening the Prince and his men rode away from Matalane, swearing Hettel would be sorry for his laughter.

At the time there was a great king whose name was Ludwig living in Normandy. His only son and heir was Hartmut, a handsome young man and a good knight. But Hartmut's mother, Lady Gerlind, had lost three sons before he was born and she was overanxious in her love for Hartmut. This made him weaker and less able to resist his mother than a man should be. Even when his sister Ortrun was born, Lady Gerlind loved Hartmut best, with a fiercely passionate love.

Now rumor flies faster than the birds, and it was not long before Lady Gerlind heard about the Prince of the Moors and his love for golden-eyed Gudrun, and about Hettel's laughter. A plan came into her mind, took root in her heart and began to grow. She watched her son in secret, and she thought he was the finest, noblest young man in the world; the longer she watched him, the surer she felt that the only girl worthy of him would be Gudrun, Princess of the Hegelings.

So she told King Ludwig her plan, urging him all day and every day to take her advice, and telling Hartmut such tales of Gudrun's golden hair that he felt he really was in love with her, even though he had never see her.

Then Gerlind ordered her chaplain to write a letter asking for Gudrun's hand. She gave her envoys clothes and rich gifts out of her own treasure to take with them, and told them to go to the land of the Hegelings.

King Ludwig was angry. "Have you never heard how Gudrun's mother was carried off from Ireland, Lady Gerlind? The Hegelings are arrogant people, and I dare say we shall do no better than the Prince of the Moors!"

"I wish I could lead a strong army to the land of the Hegelings, Mother!" said Hartmut. "I should like to fight for Gudrun, and never let go of my sword till I had won her!"

Gerlind's messengers set out, and they had a hard journey to the land of the Hegelings. They traveled for a hundred days or more, and at last they found themselves upon the coast of Denmark, where Horand held court with great splendor, though he had no wife; he never married as long as he lived. Twice a year, at Easter and Christmas, Wate and Frute, Horand and Morung, who had married Lady Hildburg, rode to Matalane, and then Horand would sing new songs to Lady Hilde and young Gudrun.

But when Horand had given Lord Hartmut's messengers food and shelter, he took them to Matalane himself, although it was midsummer and not Christmas or Easter.

King Hettel welcomed his guests, as his way was with strangers, but when he heard they had come to ask for Gudrun's hand in marriage to Hartmut his face darkened. He sent for a monk he kept at his court, a man who knew how to read, and when the monk had read Gerlind's letter to the very end Hettel said, "If Lord Horand himself had not brought you here, I can promise you I'd send you packing, gentlemen! My daughter Gudrun is too young to marry, and you may go and tell your king so."

But then Lady Hilde, who was Hagen the Wild's daughter, spoke up. "Hartmut must be mad to think of getting her for his wife!" she said. "My father, Lord Hagen of Ireland, gave his father, Lord Ludwig of Normandy, a hundred and three castles. The ceremony was at Karadein in Normandy, and that made Hagen Ludwig's overlord. Since when have the families of High Kings married vassals who owe allegiance?"

The envoys bowed and rode away. They were soon back in Normandy with their bad news.

There was an angry outburst from King Ludwig "This is what comes of taking women's advice!" he cried. "You brought this shame on us, Gerlind! Didn't I advise you against your plan from the start?"

Lady Gerlind wept bitterly. "Oh, my son!" she moaned. "If only I could have seen you married to Gudrun!"

As for young Hartmut, he took one of the messengers, a noble count, by the arm, saying quietly, "Can you tell me if you saw Hettel's daughter herself, Count?"

"I did indeed; she came down to welcome Lord Horand. Her hair is golden, her eyes are golden, and when she laughs there is a dimple in her cheek as if a child's finger had just pressed it. And her closest friends say her heart is purer than clear spring water."

"Well then," said Hartmut, "I will go and win her for myself!"

Lord Hartmut chose his very best men to go with him, and he set out. He did not give his name when he came to Matalane, and as an unknown knight he won the victory three times in the tournament. Hartmut had never fought better in his life than when Gudrun was watching him. He met her several times during the tournament, as she passed by with her ladies, and she returned his greeting kindly, but no more. However, Hartmut felt as though her mere glance burned him; he could think of nothing but Gudrun, he longed for Gudrun, and so, as it often happens, he did not see that another girl was falling in love with him. This girl was young Hildburg, daughter of Lord Morung of Frisia and Hildburg of Portugal.

One evening Hartmut sent one of his pages to Gudrun with a secret message, telling her that he was Hartmut of Normandy, and ever since he had seen her he felt he could not live without her. He begged her to let him ask for her hand in marriage again, observing all the usual customs. Gudrun listened to the page in amazement. She thought it so strange that any man should travel so far, and think of taking her from her mother and father in such a hurry, that she burst into laughter, leaning against her friend Hildburg for support in her fit of mirth. She laughed so much that she never noticed how Hildburg did not join in, as usual. Gudrun sent the page back to his master, telling him to say that she never intended to marry, she meant to stay with her dear, kind parents all her life, and Lord Hartmut would do best to go straight home to his own country of Normandy before her father Hettel found out who he was, because his envoys from Normandy had made Hettel very angry.

So Lord Hartmut rode home, heavyhearted, without telling anyone else his name.

However, before long another guest came to Matalane to try his strength in a tournament. His name was Lord Herwig of Zealand. Zealand was next to Ortland, where Irold was ruling until young Ortwin was old enough to be made a knight. Zealand was a small kingdom, but one which owed allegiance to no overlord. Until now, Herwig had thought more about fighting than women, and indeed he fought so well that Wate himself was forced to give ground before him three times. When trumpets sounded for the end of the day's jousting, Herwig was hot and thirsty. He flung down his mailshirt and his shield and began to wash off the black marks his iron helmet had left on his face. Then he ran swiftly up the steps but stood aside, bowing, as good manners demanded, to let some young girls pass.

However, their leader raised her eyes to him, and those eyes were golden as the young sea eagles he used to rob from their nests on the steep coasts of Zealand. And he thought there was a light of simple amazement in them.

Then Herwig felt so happy and lighthearted that he smiled at her, showing all his white teeth; the girl looked at him and smiled back, and her lips were like rose petals just unfurling from the bud. If one of the other girls, a small girl with curly black hair, had not drawn her away, perhaps she would have stood there longer looking at him with her golden eyes, and perhaps Herwig would have reached out his hands to her, as he reached out for the young sea eagles whose beaks were so sharp.

That evening Herwig found out that the girl was Gudrun of the Hegelings, and as soon as he got home he sent some of his men to ask for her hand in marriage. But the gifts his messengers had to offer were the least magnificent any of her suitors had brought.

Word came back to King Herwig, too, that Gudrun was too young. Herwig only smiled when he heard that.

He gathered together all his warriors, and put on his helmet over his light brown hair. He himself carried his banner, at the head of his men, and he attacked Ortland so suddenly that Lord Irold was taken by surprise. Irold's men had grown lazy during so many years of peace, it took them too long to get ready and on horseback, and Herwig was upon them almost before they knew it.

After this quick victory he went on to Matalane, riding day and night, with the men of Zealand singing in time to the beat of their horses' hooves.

They laid siege to the castle and attacked the gate, with Herwig at their head. His helmet had fallen off and his hair, light brown as his horse's mane, was blowing in the wind.

Gudrun looked down from her window and suddenly she felt that the hair around his forehead was like an angel's halo. The enemies came together, and she heard the splintering of spears. Gudrun was a true grandchild of Hagen the Wild, and the thought of a battle had never frightened her before, but now she wanted to cover that unprotected head with her own hands. Her knees trembled, and she clung to Hildburg so tight that she hurt her friend without realizing it.

"Why, do you really think he is more worth loving than Hartmut?" asked Hildburg, amazed.

Gudrun only whispered, her face pale, "They are not to kill him!"

She ran down and threw herself on her father's armed chest just as Lord Hettel was preparing to lead his men out of the gate. Trembling, she begged him to stop the fighting.

Lord Hettel saw his daughter glowing and trembling, and for the first time he realized that she was a woman now. He offered to make peace with Herwig.

"Not unless I may come before the ladies unarmed," said Lord Herwig.

So the Hegelings and the men of Zealand took off their mailshirts. Hettel himself took Herwig to the hall where the women were. When Gudrun saw the Lord of Zealand come into the hall, the blood rose in her face like crimson wine filling a goblet of milk-white onyx. Queen Hilde asked Lord Herwig to sit down, and welcomed him courteously, though she was glancing keenly at him, but as she looked at him her face gradually softened.

"I cannot offer great treasures as a bride price," said Herwig, "but perhaps what I do have to offer weighs heavier when I throw my sword into the scale. And the richest men do not always give their wives most happiness!"

He looked at the ladies, and his eyes were blue as an open flame. Then Gudrun said, softly, "Sir, surely no well-brought-up lady could be harsh enough to scorn such a good knight's love! Speak, and I will listen!"

And little Hildburg thought of poor Hartmut of Normandy, who was a good knight too and had been scorned, and thought she could never understand the strange ways of the heart.

However, Herwig rose from his seat and went up to Gudrun. Their eyes met, and once again they both thought they were so happy they must laugh out loud in wonder and amazement. Herwig's brown hands clasped Gudrun's slender ones, and the whole world around seemed to disappear.

"Then," said Lord Hettel, his voice shaking, "will you take Herwig of Zealand as your husband, Gudrun?"

She bowed her head and said, "Yes, Father—Herwig and no one else!"

So Gudrun was betrothed to Herwig with a ring and a solemn promise, though Lord Hettel insisted on putting off the wedding for a year. And as our story tells, that caused great grief and bitter suffering.

CHAPTER FOUR

The Prince of the Moors attacks Zealand
How King Hettel comes to Herwig's aid
How Gerlind advises Hartmut to carry off Gudrun
Hartmut carries Gudrun away from the land
of the Hegelings
How Wate of Sturmen took the pilgrims' ships
The great battle on the Wulpensand

When news reached the Prince of the Moors that Herwig and Gudrun had exchanged the solemn kiss of betrothal, he felt there was not room in the whole world for himself and the Lord of Zealand too.

He summoned his followers from all his lands and sailed to Zealand in his tall ships. His men attacked, laying the country waste and burning it as they went. They were fierce fighters who did not spare women or children. Brave as he was, Herwig could not do much to resist such a mighty force.

When he realized that six Moors seemed to spring up out of the ground for every one who was killed, Herwig sent messengers to Hettel, to remind him of their newly made alliance. As soon as he heard the message, Lord Hettel sent to raise his army, even before Gudrun, in tears, could beg him to do so. Before three days were up Wate was riding into the courtyard on his dapple gray, and before four days were up Horand arrived, and before five days were up wise Frute had joined them. Lord Morung, keeping his promise to Herwig, was to attack the Moors from behind.

When the Hegelings got to Zealand there was a great battle, and by nightfall many men who had been alive and laughing that morning were lying in the dust.

The Hegelings cut the Moors off from their ships and pressed them as hard as the Moors themselves had been besieging Herwig in his castle. But the Moors were brave men, and neither would yield victory to the other. Lord Hettel said he would not give in even if the fighting went on for a whole year.

At Karadein in Normandy, Lady Gerlind heard of the fighting. All this time she had been watching her son grieve for Gudrun; now she questioned the messengers who came to her closely, and at last she laughed her evil laugh.

"Lord Ludwig, this is the time to summon all your men!"

Lord Ludwig simply gave a surly growl in reply and asked what she was planning now and where she meant to stir up trouble this time.

"In the Hegelings' land!" replied wicked Gerlind. "Didn't you know that every man of them has gone to Zealand leaving the women alone to protect the castle?"

And whatever Lord Ludwig might say, she would not let him alone. She nagged and nagged at him day and night—surely his only son's whole happiness in life was worth a swordstroke or two? Until finally, sighing, Lord Ludwig gave in to her, just as he had always done over the years.

As for Gerlind, she went from man to man, promising them silver and fine gold if they would help her avenge Hettel's refusal of her son.

Since Hartmut had come home after Gudrun scorned his love, he had been like a sick man, sad and quiet, taking no interest in anything. But when he learned he was to see Gudrun again life came back into him, and he gave generous gifts to anyone who would go with him.

Lady Gerlind had the ships fitted out from the rich dowry she herself had brought to the land of Normandy as a bride, and she kissed Hartmut over and over again when he set out on his voyage.

They had a good wind and came ashore when they saw the white towers of Matalane in the distance. Lord Ludwig wanted to attack the castle at once; he was still very angry he had been made to set out on this expedition at all. But Hartmut asked his father to let him try persuading Gudrun to come with him of her own free will once more. And he sent word to tell her that rather than go home without her, he would let himself be cut to pieces here, outside the castle of Matalane.

Three great counts brought this message to Hilde and Gudrun but Hartmut's proposals of marriage were received no better this third time than before.

"I will never marry Hartmut!" cried Gudrun. "I am betrothed to Lord Herwig of Zealand and as long as I live I shall never want anyone else for my husband!"

Lady Hilde offered gifts to the three counts, but they would not take anything, and asked her permission to ride back to their ships.

Hartmut ran to meet them, and when he heard their news his lips tightened. "Did you tell her our army was standing ready outside Matalane?" he asked.

"We did, sir, just as you told us. But Lady Gudrun replied, 'If Lord Hartmut will not drink wine with us, then we must give him blood!' We never heard a sweeter mouth speak bitterer words!"

"Then the man who advises me to begin attacking Matalane is my truest friend now!" cried Lord Hartmut, eyes burning.

When the sentries saw Norman standards raised outside the fortress, Hilde told them to make haste and barricade the gate. But those men left to guard the women and the castle thought it would be shameful to lurk in safety; they chose to fasten Hettel's standards to their spears and go out to fight openly.

Once the battle started, however, with sword clashing against sword, they found Lord Ludwig's army was so strong that they were sorry they had not taken Hilde's advice.

When at last the Hegelings fled back to the castle the Normans were close on their heels, and still fighting under Lord Hartmut's banners they made their way in through the gateway.

Holding his standard in his left hand, Hartmut cut himself a way through the courtyard and the hall with his sword, until he reached the tower. Once there, he tore down Hettel's white standard and planted his own in its place. The Hegeling women began to wail bitterly, and Lady Hilde longed with all her heart for Hettel and Wate, still away in Zealand.

The Normans began to loot all the rich goods they could find, as was their custom, searching among the dead and wounded warriors. But Hartmut made his way past the Hegelings and into Gudrun's chamber. His eyes were burning in the shadow of his helmet, and his mouth was shaking as he said, "Do you still think so little of Hartmut the Norman now, lady?"

Gudrun only turned away from him. "If my father were at home," she said, "and Wate, and my beloved Herwig, you would never have dared be so cowardly and come here like thieves and murderers!"

Then Hartmut turned and gave orders, swearing by his sword blade, for all the looting to stop and the fires being lit around Matalane castle to be put out.

Ludwig was afraid the Hegelings might come back from Zealand; he wanted to get home as fast as he could. He made the Normans go back to their ships and tore Gudrun from Hilde's arms. They took sixty-two young girls on board ship with Gudrun; there was no one to stop them, and Lady Hilde wrung her hands, weeping in despair.

She saw the yellow sails of the Norman ships hoisted, she saw them grow smaller and smaller and then vanish far away over the blue horizon.

After that she sent a boy with a message; there were not many grown men left unwounded at Matalane. The lad rode day and night till he came to King Hettel and his army's camp.

Horand was the first to see Lady Hilde's colors and her messenger, who was nearly crushed as his exhausted horse collapsed. He ran up to the boy, wiped the sweat from his forehead, and offered him wine in his own golden goblet.

Then the boy opened his eyes and saw Horand's face. He sat up, and seeing all the knights around him, armed and ready for that day's fighting with the Moors, he cried in his youthful voice, which was just breaking, "Bad news, my lords! Disaster struck while you were fighting here! The castle has been attacked, the countryside burned, and Lady Gudrun and all her women stolen away!"

"It was Hartmut who did this!" cried Herwig, tears in his eyes, his brown fists clenched. "Oh, if only you had let her marry me at once, when I begged you to do so!"

"We must keep the news secret," said Wate, "or the Prince of the Moors will attack us more fiercely than ever."

"By no means, my friend Wate!" said Frute. "I shall tell him the news myself, and at once!" And seeing how surprised all the warriors were, wise Frute said, "We need peace with the Prince of the Moors now, and more than peace. If he is told of Gudrun's abduction in the right way, he will help us rescue her!"

They saw the Prince of the Moors riding toward them already, impatient to start fighting. He was at the head of his army, his leopard skin floating out in the wind, and the red scarf bound round his golden helmet blazed like a spurt of flame in the sun. His horse's harness was all gold, the horse itself was gray like the clouds, and it could go faster than the clouds.

Lord Frute ordered the horns to be blown and Irold of Waleis called out, his voice echoing above his lowered shield like the bellowing of a bull, "Prince of the Moors, will you make peace with the Hegelings?"

The Prince of the Moors stopped short in mid-career, reining in his horse so that it reared up, and then he lowered his spear with its standard.

"I will only make peace if it can be done honorably," he said warily.

"We are asking you to act honorably indeed," replied Frute. "We ask you to help us go after the man who has carried Lady Gudrun away."

The Moor's brown face twisted savagely below his golden helmet, and he hissed through his white teeth, "Who is this man?" They told him Hartmut's name, and on hearing it he uttered a curse in a language none of them understood. He put his sword and the swords of all his men at the Hegelings' service against Hartmut, for great misfortune, as they say, makes men forget smaller grievances.

So they made up their quarrel and they all discussed how best to catch up with the robbers. Wate offered to lead them in the pursuit.

But Hettel shook his head regretfully. "We set out

for a campaign on land, and only the Moors have ships. How can we follow Ludwig?"

Wate laughed till his whole body shook. "This time, my lord, Wate can play the wise counselor!" he said. "Last night I saw some hundred ships carrying pilgrims, anchored in a bay. The good pilgrims can't be in such a hurry to reach the Holy Land . . . they may wait here on shore until we come back with their ships!"

And though Lord Frute did not like this idea at all, there was plainly no other way to catch up with the Normans.

Lord Wate set out with a hundred men. He offered the pilgrims large sums of money but they said they would not part with their ships. Then Wate lost his temper and would not take no for an answer, loud as the pilgrims complained. He had all their valuables and provisions unloaded from the ships, hauled in the anchors, hoisted the sails with their signs of the Cross, and came sailing back to Hettel, smiling broadly.

When King Ludwig reached a desolate harbor called the Wulpensand he thought that at last it was safe to stop and rest. They had sailed as fast as they could, both day and night, and the women were tired to death.

The Normans lit camp fires and their beautiful hostages sank down beside the fires to weep for their sad fate. Except for one of them, the lovely Duchess Heregart, who began replaiting her hair, which glowed like copper in the firelight, and talked to the Normans standing near.

Lord Ludwig had been urging them to go fast all the time until they reached the Wulpensand, but now he thought they might allow themselves seven days' rest since he knew very well that Hettel was far away, fighting other enemies, and had no ships with him. He liked the thought of a little respite between the fighting at Matalane and his return home to his sharp-tongued wife.

However, they had not been three nights on the Wulpensand when Lord Hartmut, walking on the beach, saw ships coming up with the sign of the cross on their sails. He thought it was strange that pilgrim ships should be steering such a northerly course, and looking more closely he sighted men on deck who, he felt sure, had never worn pilgrims' crosses on their clothes.

Hartmut ran back as fast as he could, shouting out to the men lying idly around, "My sword, my sword! Our enemies are coming!"

By now the ships were so near that it was too late for the Normans to drive them back by throwing spears from the shore: they would have to fight at close quarters.

Wate was the first to leap ashore, with darts flying around him as thick as snowflakes on the wintry Alps. Soon the Normans saw Wate had lost none of his famous strength. A great bank began rising by the sea, built of the bodies of Norman and Hegeling warriors, for the battle was fiercest down at the waves' edge. Herwig could find nowhere to tie up his ships, since the other ships were standing so close together, so he leaped from deck to deck and then flung himself into the sea in his shirt of mail. Half wading, half swimming, he made his way through the floating bodies, surrounded by a hail of darts, and when he felt sea water on his lips it did not seem bitter and salty but sweetish with the taste of blood.

Hartmut flung a spear at him but Herwig avoided it nimbly. He and his followers made their way over to join the Hegelings and take the place of the fallen men. Many good warriors died there; blood stained the rough sea water, floating on it like oil, and sea swallows darted to and fro above the clashing swords, screeching and circling over the cliffs where they nested in alarm.

Though the Normans had acted like thieves at Matalane, they fought like heroes on the Wulpensand, standing firm even before the Moors with their weird battle cries and sharp, curved scimitars. At the spot where they had placed the hostages for safety they stood in ranks ten deep; if Herwig struck one man down, three more leaped into the gap to take his place, and the Hegelings could not get through to the women. They could only hear their weeping. Even in death, the corpses of the Normans made a wall around them, a wall growing higher all the time.

The Hegelings fought from dawn to the heat of midday, they fought on from midday to the cool of evening, and by then the fine sand of the seashore was soaked and thickened with blood.

The Hegelings still fought on until it began to get too dark to be sure if they were striking friends or enemies. But as dusk fell, Hettel and Ludwig met in the battle and they fought for a long time. Hettel was making his way closer and closer to Gudrun, and it looked as though he would soon rescue his daughter. He could already see her golden hair. Then Ludwig struck him a mighty blow on the head, and the blow went home.

Gudrun saw her father fall and cried out, trying to break through the iron ring of guards with her own tender hands, battering her fists against their shields and armed backs. But the ring of Normans stood firm, even when Wate rushed to the attack.

"For Hettel! For Hettel!" shouted Wate, with every stroke that felled a man. He thought that cry the best lament of all for Hettel's death. Many Hegelings and many Normans died at the same time as King Hettel.

At last it was so dark that they could scarcely see their own sword blades. Then they left off fighting, and the survivors lit fires. The light shone strangely in the eyes of the dead men.

Ludwig came in secret to his son, who was sleeping the sleep of exhaustion, and woke him.

"Tomorrow you will see Wate kill me," said the king.

"God forbid, Father—God and my sword!" said Hartmut.

"If we wait here until morning, neither yours nor any other sword can prevent it! Wate will come to kill me then."

"We cannot have it said that we Normans ran away from the Hegelings by night!" cried Hartmut.

"And Gudrun?" asked Lord Ludwig. "Do you think so little of your prize that you risk it now?"

Then Hartmut groaned, and buried his face in his hands.

Ludwig, however, went about telling his men to make a great deal of noise around their camp fires. Then, when the Hegelings fell asleep and their own camp fires were gradually dying down, the Normans secretly took the women on board ship, threatening to throw anyone who screamed into the sea. When they had them all on board, the Normans saw that many of their ships must be left behind empty, because so many men had died on the Wulpensand.

So they put out to sea at dead of night, taking the sobbing girls with them, and by the time day came they were far away.

When the first rosy light of dawn appeared in the sky, Wate woke and blew his great horn. The Hegelings staggered to their feet, stretching, faces still heavy with sleep, their eyes bleary and their eyelids like lead. The wounded got to their feet too, and men who were tired to death; half asleep, they all reached for their weapons, mounted their weary horses and drew up in battle order, though there was scarcely room because so many men still lay there on the ground—men who could never be wakened again even by Wate's horn.

Wate blew his horn till the veins stood out at his temples, challenging the enemy to come and fight. But the Normans were quiet as the dead men lying in the sand.

"I thought they had more ships than that, anchored out at sea," said Frute.

The Hegelings stared at him, hardly daring to guess at what they saw in his face.

Spies, creeping up to those Norman ships still lying at anchor, found them empty. Abandoned weapons were strewn around the beach, among the cold camp fires and the piles of dead. The spies came running back as fast as they could, shouting out loud that the Normans were gone. Herwig went pale to the lips and covered his eyes with his hands.

"On board! On board!" cried Wate, and the Hegelings leaped out of their saddles, armor clashing.

But Lord Horand, who knew Frute well, raised his hand. As he stood there Frute had pulled up a sprig of heather, and was holding it up to the brisk breeze that was blowing. He glanced in turn from the sky to the sea, its white-crested waves breaking against the rocks.

Looking at Herwig with kindness in his eyes, Frute said, "It's a hard fate to see farther than other men. And I see three things, but you will not thank me for telling you!

"First: they must have sailed some thirty miles before we even woke! The wind and the tide were in their favor.

"Second: they are going home to their own peaceful country, where they will find plenty of men to replace the Normans we have killed.

"Third: we need food, and we need weapons, and we have lost many of our own men, fighting in Zealand and then here yesterday. This is what I see. Now, tell me yourselves, what advice should I give you?"

Herwig seized his arm and shook it, crying out, "Frute, for the sake of Christ's Passion, have you thought what you are advising us to do?"

Frute placed both hands on Herwig's shoulders, saying sadly, "I am advising you to do the most difficult thing in the world for a brave man, Herwig: to give up the idea of following on your enemies' trail to take revenge!"

All the Hegelings murmured. None of them looked sleepy now; their swords glittered in the cold morning light as they turned them downward, a custom of the Hegelings ever since ancient times when their own hearts did not agree with what their leader said.

Wate, flushed with rage, came face to face with Frute

and cried, "Is this the loyalty we all swore to our overlord, Hettel? Shall we sit warm by our own firesides without avenging a crime so shameful it cries out to heaven?"

"Do not think only of your own wishes, Wate," said Frute sadly. "Look around you."

Wate looked at the men standing beside him. And though every one of them raised his sword now, there were not so very many blades to reflect the sunlight. Every shield and helmet was battered, no one had escaped wounds. Wate's lips began to tremble under his gray beard when he saw that the company of dead Hegelings lying there around Hettel was far larger than the living army.

Then Wate knelt down in front of them all: Wate, who was so proud that even Hettel had allowed him to pay homage standing. He prayed out loud, "Dear Lord, is this my puunishment for harming your servants? It pierces me to the heart! Lord God, I am an old man! Strike me with your lightning, here on my knees, but do not ask me to go home to Lady Hilde with this news!"

There was utter silence as they looked up at the blue sky. Frute bent, and gently helped his friend up from his knees. Lord Horand said, in his clear voice, "I can see nothing for it but to take Frute's advice. May God forgive us, we must go back home."

And he sheathed his sword. The harsh sound was painful to hear in the silence.

Without a word, Morung and Irold and Herwig copied him.

Then their followers bowed their heads and sheathed their own swords too, with hands trembling so much they could hardly get the blades into the sheaths. Many of them slid down from their faithful horses and hid their faces in the manes so that no one would see their bitter tears. The horses pawed the ground and twisted their heads back, nuzzling and snuffling at their masters' arms, as if asking a gentle question.

The sun stood high in the sky above the living men, sad and powerless now, and above those who had found peace.

Then Herwig said, voice shaking, "Gudrun?" He put his hands to his temples, shaking his head as if to escape the thoughts that swarmed like wasps around him; then he turned and staggered away, stumbling and tottering like a blind man. But one man followed him, a man who knew how tears shed alone can burn the heart.

In his despair, Herwig had forgotten all words but Gudrun's name. The singer Horand spoke to him, showing Herwig his own heart's wounds, which had never healed and which he had kept hidden for so many years. "You see, a man can bear these things and yet endure to live," he said, comforting Herwig.

Frute, who knew that hard work is the best cure for deep grief, asked the Hegelings, "Will you leave your good king and all your comrades to the foxes and ravens? We must dig them a grave and raise a stone memorial above it."

So Hettel and all the Hegelings were buried, with much honor, and a huge monument of stones was piled above the grave, in memory of that great battle. When this was done, they took Frute's wise advice again and buried the Normans too.

White-robed priests, who had heard of the battle on the Wulpensand, came to raise their right hands and bless the dead. They blessed the living too, for burying their enemies honorably.

"We sinned when we took the holy pilgrims' ships," said Frute. "Sin brings its own punishment, so now we will do penance."

The Hegelings sold the dead men's weapons and horses, and gave all their own silver and gold for the white monks to build a church and pray there for the souls of the men buried on the Wulpensand. One of the priests thrust his cross into the ground and consecrated the place before the Hegelings left.

They sailed slowly away. The wind that had favored the Normans made their own sails hang slack against the masts. They sat at the oars, bareheaded, and no one spoke a word as long as they could still see the white memorial on the Wulpensand, far away.

* * *

Hoar frost was falling as they reached their own shores. No one shouted for joy, no one so much as smiled to see his own country again.

"And now for the hardest thing of all," said Wate, quietly. "I will be the man to take Lady Hilde the news. That shall be my penance for driving the holy pilgrims off their ships by force."

When Horand offered to go with him he shook his head obstinately, for Lord Wate could be as hard to himself as he was with others.

They saw him mount his dapple-gray stallion, laying his spear over the saddle. It no longer carried his overlord's colors: Wate wore Hettel's bloodstained standard on his heart, under his shirt of mail.

He began to ride, slowly. Ravens strutted ahead of him over the frosty fields, and the slow tread of his horse's hooves did not send them flying up.

Wate sat in the saddle, head bent. He had taken the braid out of his gray hair, and it hung in tangles, the gray mixed with white. As he left his companions, they thought for the first time that Wate looked an old man.

The people in Matalane saw a lonely horseman approaching, and thought nothing of it. Wate himself always used to come home with banners waving and horns blowing, much noise and a great retinue.

It was only when the dogs, barking and whining breathlessly, came rushing up to him, chasing back and forth, their paws wet from the path and their damp muzzles nuzzling him, that the sentry's cry rang out to announce his arrival.

"I cannot see any men with Wate and I do not hear his horn. Are my poor eyes too dim with tears to see Hettel's standard?" asked Lady Hilde.

Her women, afraid, said they could not see the standard either.

"Then God have mercy upon us!" breathed Lady Hilde, clasping her son Ortwin close to her.

People began running through the courtyards and the passages, down the stairs, making for the gateway. All eyes strained to see Wate's face.

The old man gritted his teeth.

"I am a poor hand at pretence, Lady Hilde; I cannot hide the truth from you. Our best men all lie dead. I wish I were not the bringer of such news!"

They were all stricken, not daring to ask questions. They clung to the walls for support, as sad a company as was ever seen.

"So I have lost them both," said Queen Hilde, into the stricken silence. "Both Hettel and my child!"

"Do not cry, Mother!" begged handsome young Ortwin. "I will go with Wate and we will soon kill Hartmut and bring back my sister Gudrun!" Once the boy had spoken, there was no one there who would not have urged Wate to set out for Normandy at once.

But Wate, who knew how many men were buried on the Wulpensand better than they did, was silent as he began to take stock of the Hegelings and their weapons.

Lord Hettel's huge armories were empty. The storehouses for provisions were bare after so many months of war. And when he counted the warriors standing there in the castle courtyard of Matalane, there were hardly a thousand. Wate thought that Lord Frute had been right, and the last spark of hope in his heart went out.

He went up to Lady Hilde in the great hall, and when she looked at him as if he were to pronounce judgment between life and death, he drew a deep breath.

"Lady, we have suffered great misfortune and it was my sin which brought us bad luck. I drove the holy pilgrims off their ships, to take them and pursue the Normans, and I did not pay them anything."

Lady Hilde took the handkerchief from her shaking mouth and cried, in her grief, "Go and take the ships back to the good pilgrims and pay every one of them three marks of silver! Those who harm God's servants harm God himself!"

Next morning the rest of the Hegeling army came filing in, slowly and silently, with no shouting or blowing of horns. They were tired and sad, and many badly wounded. Lady Hilde gazed at the exhausted men with eyes that had no tears left to shed.

The warriors sat in the castle hall, pale and heavy-eyed, and no one had a word to say. They simply stared at their empty hands, so that they need not look into Hilde's eyes. Then Lord Frute rose, slowly. "The only advice I can give you, lady, is what you are afraid to hear. We must wait. Boys must grow up to be men here in our own country, men who can fight. Children orphaned on the Wulpensand must be old enough to be made knights before we can think of revenge." And he laid his hand on Ortwin's fair head.

Lady Hilde raised her face under its widow's coif and it was pale as wax. They could all see how tears had drowned her beauty. "My heart does not cry out for revenge. If you were to kill every man in Normandy, you could not bring my husband back to life! I am thinking of my child and what she must be suffering. Shall I ever hold Gudrun in my arms again?"

On his knees before her, Lord Herwig said, "You have not lost all your avengers, lady! May God forsake me at the hour of my death if I ever forget the oath I swear now!"

"I am growing old," said Frute, "and I think sleep can never rid me of the weariness I have felt since I held my dead lord in my arms. But I hope I shall not go to God's peace before I can bring Gudrun back to you." And all the heroes swore the same oath, one by one; the Prince of the Moors swore it too, on the blade of his curved sword.

Last to kneel was Lord Horand. He looked at Lady

Hilde with the sad smile of those who understand loneliness.

"I have had one comfort in my life, and now I swear on my sword to give that up. I will sing no more songs until I see you kiss Lady Gudrun."

Next day the heroes asked quietly for permission to go home, and Lady Hilde sent them back to their own lands. Their horses were led out of the stables, with dogs snapping and barking around their hooves, and servants running and shouting. Then the friends mounted. Their parting was bitter.

Riding down the winding path, the knights could see Lady Hilde's black veil wave in the wind as the ravens fluttered around the white towers of Matalane.

CHAPTER FIVE

*How the Normans sailed away from the Wulpensand
Lord Hartmut saves Gudrun from drowning
How Gudrun refused Lady Gerlind's kiss
Gudrun is made to tend the fires in Karadein castle
How Hartmut found Gudrun there on his return*

The Normans sailed away from the Wulpensand as fast as they could go, setting men to keep a lookout all the time. But the Hegelings did not seem to be coming after them. There were some of them who muttered discontentedly and felt more ashamed of this flight than of anything they had ever done before, thinking that Lord Ludwig was not coming home from the Wulpensand with much honor.

They had many wounded men who were laid in the holds where they would feel the rolling of the sea less. Their groaning and feverish cries were loud both by day and by night, and so was the women's weeping. It made the Normans sick at heart and they exchanged bitter words.

But one day the lookouts sighted the great castles of Normandy in their setting of the silvery sea and the dark forests. Then all the Normans felt cheered and shouts of joy rang out from ship to ship; they climbed the rigging, pointing to land and wondering whether the white shape they thought they saw at a window was only a sheet—or was it a woman looking out for their return?

They carried their wounded companions down the narrow gangplanks on their backs, and the wounded themselves, who had feared they would go to feed the fishes, raised themselves as best they could, supported by their swords, to see their beloved land of Normandy, laughing as if they were well again.

But the laments of the poor hostages grew louder. They clustered around Gudrun, gazing, terrified, at these strange castles that seemed to reach right up to the cloudy sky. They felt that their ship was like sun and shade at once: their own grief mingling with the Normans' delight in getting home.

King Ludwig of Normandy himself came on board the

hostages' ship to welcome Gudrun to his own country. When Ludwig was happy, he did not like to have weeping women around him. He smiled, pointing his large hand at the level beaches and the fishermen's cottages, their straw thatch looking like a warm cap pulled down over the ears. There were wide pastures, reaching far back inland, where the heavy Norman cattle, their black coats flecked with amber spots, grazed knee-deep in the tall, wet, emerald-green grass. But Gudrun had no eyes for the rich pastures and golden fields. All she saw was the two castles, Kassiane and Karadein, rising high above the land, each with its mighty defensive ramparts. Many enemies had learned their strength and regretted it. When she saw those great towers she knew all the might of the Hegelings would be crushed between them like corn ground between millstones.

"Well, Lady Gudrun, and how do you like the land of Normandy?" asked Lord Ludwig, smiling. "There are not many fairer countries on the earth! If you will be friends with us, you shall have joy and honor here, and give our fair land good heirs!"

Gudrun opened her eyes, and there was not much goodwill to be seen in them. She would not touch the outstretched hand that had shed her father's blood. "Unfortunate I may be," she said, "but how could I ever be friends with you, now that God has turned away from me? My life is all turned to sorrow!"

Ludwig found it hard not to show anger. "Is it really such a misfortune to live in Kassiane and be loved by Lord Hartmut?" he asked. "My son is considered a brave knight, Lady Gudrun!"

At that, everyone watching could see that young Gudrun was the true grandchild of Hagen. She flung back her head, and golden sparks seemed to spring from her eyes. "I'd sooner be dead and buried than take Hartmut for my husband! If anyone foretold by his cradle that he was to mingle his blood with that of the High Kings, then I never heard of it!"

Ludwig's face went as red as his cloak. Gudrun's voice rang so bitterly in his ears that he forgot the courtesy a man should always show to women. He pushed her so hard that she staggered, slipped on the wet deck, and fell into the sea.

Lord Hartmut was talking to his wounded companions. Gudrun's cry brought him to his feet in time to see her sink. He dropped what was in his hands and jumped into the sea himself, fully armed.

As Gudrun rose, to sink again for the second time, he managed to catch hold of the end of her plaited hair, and he pulled her in, unconscious, as if he were bringing in some rare fish on the end of a golden line.

He reached a little dinghy tied to the ship, laid his motionless burden in the craft, which was almost capsizing, hauled himself in, too, and began to unfasten

Gudrun's dripping clothes. He raised and lowered her bare arms, where beaded drops of water hung quivering like dew on flower petals and, though he was shivering with cold himself, he did not stop until Gudrun began to breathe again. She came back to her senses, sat upright in the rocking boat, saw that she was in her wet shift, and felt ashamed; she was not used to such treatment. The other girls were all weeping with terror for their mistress and for their own fate; every one of them feared for her own safety if this was the way the Normans treated their princess.

Hartmut picked Gudrun up in his arms and took her back to her ladies on the ship. Hildburg hurried to put her own cloak around her. Then Lord Hartmut, very angry, went up to his father. "Do you want to drown my bride, when you know I love her ten times better than my own life? If it had been any man but you, Father, I'd take both his life and his honor now!"

Ludwig muttered into his beard. "I've lived an honorable life and I hope to live honorably till I die, so ask Lady Gudrun to forgive me, my son." But he was thinking to himself that women caused all the trouble in the world.

Hartmut sent a messenger to his mother, asking her to get ready to receive Gudrun, because now the girl he had longed for even before he saw her was landing in Normandy, and he would like Lady Gerlind and his young sister Ortrun to come down to the shore to welcome his bride to Karadein.

When Lady Gerlind got his message she thought she had never heard better news in all her life. "I shall be more than happy to do as Lord Hartmut asks!" she cried. "I will welcome Hettel's daughter with all honor. She need not think she has come to any place unworthy of her."

Young Ortrun was delighted, too; she could hardly wait to see Gudrun and find out if she was really as lovely as the wandering minstrels sang.

And on the third morning, everything was ready to welcome the Normans and the captive women.

The warriors who guarded the two castles led Lady Gerlind and a noble retinue down to the sea. Young Ortrun rode out ahead of them all, on her little Irish horse with the tiny silver bells woven into its thick mane, a prince of Normandy on either side of her. Her clear eyes glanced around, wondering which of the women—and there were over sixty of them—might be Gudrun. Then she saw her beloved brother Hartmut leading a girl by the hand; the girl's head was bent so that the plaits of her hair were cast forward and reached down to her feet. Ortrun saw that her hair was the color of wild honey: so this was Gudrun! The girls who followed her were sobbing bitterly, and suddenly young Ortrun realized that her own country, which she loved so dearly, was a strange and alien place to them. She dismounted from her horse and ran to meet the hostages. Slowly, Gudrun raised her eyes; she saw Ortrun's small, troubled face, and smiled. Ortrun knew at once she would love her forever. She flung her arms around Gudrun's neck and kissed her, feeling that she knew in her heart that Gudrun was perfect and she could not wish her to be different in any way.

Then they helped Lady Gerlind down from the saddle. When she saw King Hagen's grandchild beside her son she drew a deep breath. She bent to kiss Gudrun, but before her thin lips could touch Gudrun's cheek the girl drew back.

"I will never take your kiss, lady! This wicked raid was your doing. You were the one who sent these knights to bring me to such misery!"

Lady Gerlind was secretly angry, but she kept her anger to herself, and pretended to be kind and loving all the same.

As for the common people of Normandy, both men and women, and all the servants who greeted Gudrun by the wayside, she smiled kindly back at them, and they thought they had never seen anyone so sweet and beautiful in their land before.

The Hegeling women wept all the way to Ludwig's castle. All but one, the Duchess Heregart, whose hair was redder than a red squirrel's coat and whose skin was white as a squirrel's breast: she was exchanging glances with Gerlind's handsome cupbearer. Seeing that, little Hildburg wept even harder than before, because she had loved Heregart.

Gudrun stood in the courtyard, watching them carry in the goods looted from her father's castle, and hearing them barter the stuff, priding themselves on their rich takings, and she thought her heart would break.

Hartmut saw her pain, and led her courteously to the rooms his mother had set aside for her. Gudrun spent the night there with her ladies, in great fear and grief.

Next day Gerlind asked her, "And when shall we hold the wedding? It will be a happy day; I'm sure any girl might be glad to get a husband like Lord Hartmut!"

Gudrun listened. "Tell me, lady," she said, quietly and sadly, "would you yourself have been glad of a husband who had brought so much sorrow on those you loved?"

"Do you think I'd have chosen Lord Ludwig for myself? What can't be cured must be endured, as they say," replied wicked Gerlind. "And if you will be Lord Hartmut's wife, why, I'll give you my own crown with all its jewels!"

"I do not want your crown, and I will not marry Lord Hartmut. I shall not stay long in Normandy! I shall be wishing for my home, day and night," said Gudrun.

When Lord Hartmut heard this, a blush of shame rose

to his cheeks. "Mother," he said unhappily, "if Gudrun likes me so little, I will not go on trying to win her love." When Gerlind saw Gudrun had given her son such pain, she was filled with hatred; she had difficulty in stopping herself leaping at Gudrun like a tigress defending her young. But she followed Hartmut and talked to him cunningly.

"Those who will not learn must be taught by older, wiser folk," she said. "Leave Gudrun to me, and I will soon bring her around and get her to speak more kindly to you."

Hartmut liked the sound of that. "Yes, Mother," he said. "But remember that everything here is strange to her, and treat her well."

When Lord Hartmut went back to his own castle of Kassiane, opposite his father's castle of Karadein, wicked Gerlind came straight to Gudrun. She faced the girl, arms folded, glaring at her angrily from narrowed eyes. "Well, if you do not want happiness, you shall have suffering instead," she laughed. "I am to decide what happens to you now, and there is no one here to shield you. Since you would not be queen, you shall work as a servant girl from now on, split and carry wood and rake out my fire." And when Gerlind had said this she waited, greed in her eyes, expecting to see Gudrun fall at her feet in tears, begging for mercy.

But Gudrun was the daughter of Hagen the Wild;

she did not flinch when she heard the wife of her grandfather's vassal give her work that was usually done only by the lowest of the maidservants. She folded her slim hands, the lovely hands of which the minstrels sang, and she smiled in Gerlind's face.

"I will be glad to do as you wish, lady, until it pleases God to ease my pain! I have never tended fires before, but I'd far rather tend yours than wear your son's crown!"

When Gerlind saw that this threat had no effect on Gudrun either, such fury welled up in her that she could happily have killed the girl. "I will humble your pride yet!" she cried. "Your fate will be one that princesses seldom have to suffer. From tomorrow you shall be parted from your retinue. All your women will be my servants, and so will you. You think yourself too good for this place, do you? I'll see to it that you get no more fine living!"

Gerlind slammed the door and marched away, her costly robes rustling. She talked to herself, clenching her fists and muttering disjointed words, and went to see Hartmut.

"Let me tell you," she said to Hartmut, "Hettel's daughter thinks less of you than she does of our gray wolfhounds, for she stroked *them*. But I'll break her pride sooner than she thinks."

Hartmut took his mother's hand. "She is very young," he said. "However proudly she may act, I beg you to be kind to her, for my sake! I love her so much, yet I have done her nothing but harm."

However, Lady Gerlind was both wicked and very sure of herself. After seeing Gudrun's smile, she did not think she could ever get her to marry Hartmut except by force. "Gudrun is obstinate; it will take firm treatment to bring her around," said she.

Hartmut replied sadly, "In that case, this is no place for me now; I will go out on another voyage with my men, as far as our ships will carry me. But Mother, once again I beg you to be my friend; be good to Gudrun, so that she will not think of me entirely as an enemy when I come back!"

This made Lady Gerlind hate Gudrun worse than ever, for letting such love go unrewarded and driving Hartmut away from home. Ludwig had never thought much of women, spending his time in sleeping and hunting—and perhaps Lady Gerlind herself might have been different if any man had ever loved her as her son loved Gudrun, though his love was not returned.

She flung open the door of the women's quarters and drove Gudrun's ladies to work, lashing them with words as well picked to hurt as if they were birch rods soaked in water. They were the daughters of dukes, of kings and of counts, but she set them to work carrying water, washing fleeces, spinning, or combing flax all day, until their soft hands were roughened and cracked. And she parted girls who had been friends since early childhood from each other, so that though they still slept in the same quarters they could hardly manage to exchange a word as they hurried through the castle corridors.

All this time, however much Gerlind tormented her, Gudrun did the servant's work she was given without a murmur, and Gerlind never saw her weep. One other Hegeling girl did not weep either; that was the Duchess Heregart. She was not set to work like the others, but sat at Gerlind's table beside the handsome cupbearer. And when Gudrun knelt to blow up the fire Heregart laughed till the wine ran down her throat the wrong way and set her coughing.

Day followed day, each with its petty torments, and night followed night, each with its secret tears. And so three and a half years passed sadly by.

Then Hartmut's ships came into harbor and lay at anchor, rocking on the water. They were crammed with goods looted from foreign lands. Hartmut himself was a finer-looking man than ever when he came back, tanned from the southern sun. And two pairs of eyes thought him even handsomer than before: the eyes of Lady Gerlind, and of a young, black-haired girl who let out a shrill cry and took to her heels when she suddenly saw Hartmut there, leaving bits of gray hemp behind her. This was not the welcome Hartmut had dreamed of all these years. He strode from room to room, flinging open door after door, calling Gudrun's name. The old castle was built in the Norman way, with its outer walls and ramparts made of stone blocks, but the inner halls were built of wood, and they echoed under his lonely tread. Gudrun's name, too, came echoing back to him from every dark corner. He did not find her in the castle halls nor in the fine chambers where he had left her. He went on, faster and faster, not daring to ask any questions, because he read bad news in the frightened faces of those he met, and he began to be afraid his beloved Gudrun was dead.

Then Hartmut of Normandy began to walk quietly and slowly, knowing in his heart that he had spent three years fighting and winning battles just to see her smile when he came back. He went down a long, narrow passage, a shortcut to his mother's apartments which he had used since childhood. It was quiet and dark here, because the windows were still boarded up to keep out the winter cold. The fires on the hearths of the queen's apartments were kindled and tended from outside the rooms, in this passage, and here among oak logs and tree roots knelt a girl with hair as golden as Gudrun's. As Hartmut stood there, unable to believe his eyes, she said softly, "You see, my lord, this is how you find me."

Lord Hartmut, groaning, pulled her up from her knees. "What will become of us all?" he cried. "What has happened, lady, while I was away at sea?"

"Your mother did this," said Gudrun. "And if I am made to tend her fires, the sin is yours and the shame is mine."

When Hartmut heard her voice, warmth ran through his veins; he felt all her old magic again. Even in her sooty clothes she seemed as lovely as ever, and his burning wish to kiss her mouth, just once, was even stronger than the wise decision he had made three years before to win her love by tender thoughtfulness.

"Please stand aside," said Gudrun, bending to pick up the heavy basket of wood. "Your mother Gerlind will be angry if I let the fire go out."

In silence, Hartmut pushed her out of the way and picked up the basket of logs, which had taken all her strength to lift, as if it were light as a feather. He carried it to the fireplace and emptied it into the flames.

Then Hartmut burst into his mother's chambers; he found her in the very room whose fire Gudrun was tending outside. It was warm and bright in here, with thick furs on the floor and woven tapestries on the walls showing colored pictures of hunts and sea voyages. Gerlind and young Ortrun, who welcomed her brother home with delight, were sitting on low seats at an embroidery frame, skillfully embroidering the bishop's new cape with gold thread.

Hartmut sent his sister out of the room and cried, quite beside himself with rage and fury, "Mother, how could you insult Gudrun like this? I left her in your keeping!"

Gerlind got to her feet, eyes flashing. "You ask favors for her, do you? She asks none for herself! It was her own choice. She's at liberty to wear the crown of Normandy instead!"

Hartmut strode up and down the room, his mailshirt clashing, his spurs clanking, and his cloak, still mud-stained from his ride, swirling about him.

"Have you forgotten what we did to her? My father killed hers. I myself killed many of her friends. She did not come willingly to a foreign land; do you think you will get her to love me by heaping injustices on her?"

Lady Gerlind came up to him. Watching his face, she said harshly, "If you are so softhearted, my son, why not send her back to the Hegelings? You should know by now that however much you may want her, even if you, and I, and Lord Ludwig, and all our men were to kneel before her for thirty years, you will never, *never* truly get her love."

At that Hartmut went pale as a shroud. Lady Gerlind had never seen him look so pale before. Seeing his eyes, she made herself smile and added quickly, "But perhaps I may be wrong! For your sake, I will try kindness again!"

Hartmut went away, disturbed and restless in his mind. He spent weeks out in the forests of Normandy, hunting bears and wolves with his father, while Gerlind treated

Gudrun as harshly as ever. She had hoped her son might forget Gudrun and fall in love with other women on his voyages, and now she cursed the golden-haired girl who had caused him such sorrow. She went to Gudrun, slammed her fist down on the table, and ordered Hagen's grandchild to undo her hair and use it to wipe the dust from the tables and benches.

"I will do it!" said Gudrun, with that smile of hers which was worse than poison to Gerlind. "I will do it willingly so long as I may remain true to my beloved Herwig."

And she undid her golden hair, which seemed to cast a soft light in the room, and wiped the tables and benches with it.

When the two kings of Normandy came back from their long hunt, there was a banquet. As the noblemen sat drinking, they said it was time for Hartmut to be crowned, since he was ruling the land, and they said it was time he married Gudrun, too; then they could both be crowned on the wedding day. Hartmut thought of a decision he had made in the quiet of the forests: he would bring matters to a head. He sent asking Gudrun to let him speak to her.

A message came back from Gudrun saying it was not right for the King of Normandy to visit her in the maidservants' quarters. She came to him herself, just as she was, in her shabby clothes. And though Hartmut had seen many beautiful women on his voyages, his heart had never beaten so fast as now, when Gudrun came over to his castle of Kassiane.

He welcomed her and took her hand, and the words he had gone over a thousand times came tumbling out of his mouth. "Lady Gudrun, you must agree to be my wife, at long last, and wear the crown of Normandy!"

With a touch of proud scorn he had not seen before around her soft mouth, Gudrun said, "I have little inclination for it, my lord. I have learned to know your mother too well. She has so tired me out with work that I do not feel much like kisses."

"I will make it all up to you," said Hartmut, softly and passionately. "I will love you so much that you will forget everything that has happened."

Gudrun stepped back from him. "I can never give you my heart," she said earnestly. "Not now, nor ever!"

Hartmut came close to her, saying, "Gudrun, you know that you are in my castle, on my own land, and all my men have sworn to obey me. Who would dare have me hanged, according to the law, if I forced you to become my mistress now?"

Gudrun looked fearlessly back at him with her golden eyes. "Need I fear such wickedness from you? Your name would be dishonored if other kings were to hear you kept Hagen the Wild's granddaughter as your mistress!"

Hartmut fell on one knee: he felt he could not breathe without Gudrun. "Why should I care what they say, if only you would love me, Gudrun!"

"But I shall never love you! All my unhappiness is your doing. If I were a man, I would challenge you and King Ludwig to fight!"

Then Hartmut sprang up, so bitterly angry that now he only wanted to hurt her in any way he could. "If you have been badly treated so far, it was not by my wish! But now I do not care what happens to you! If you despise my throne and my heart, you must take the consequences."

Gudrun spread her arms wide. "I will bear that, as I have borne it all. I have been serving wicked Gerlind ever since God forgot me, and it seems I shall go on serving her still!"

Hartmut left the room in a raging fury, but as soon as he had slammed the doors behind him his anger melted away, as he thought of that one moment when she stood there laughing, arms outstretched to accept her fate—the arms that would never be flung around him.

CHAPTER SIX

*How Gudrun and Hildburg washed clothes
for Hartmut's men
Lady Hilde shows Frute the treasures of the Hegelings
Lord Herwig and Lord Ortwin*

In the evening Hartmut went to see his young sister Ortrun, and standing before her he saw that she was beginning to grow from a child to a pretty young woman. Hesitantly, and asking many questions, he begged Ortrun to help him make Gudrun forget her grief. If she succeeded, he said, he would give her many wonderful jewels and robes he had brought home from foreign lands.

"I shall be glad to go to her, and I'll help you with all

my heart," said Ortrun. "I have felt so sorry for her all this time. I will bow to her myself and all my ladies shall serve her as if they were her own."

So Gudrun was brought to Ortrun's room, and Hartmut's young sister offered her red wine; it was a long time since Gudrun had tasted wine. And when the delicate color rose to her cheeks, Ortrun thought her so beautiful she could not stop looking at her. But as Ortrun talked she suddenly began to cry, and Gudrun took her in her arms to comfort her. Through her tears, the girl said how much she wanted Gudrun for her sister-in-law, and asked if Hartmut was so very dreadful, and would Gudrun always force people who were not really unkind to treat her harshly? Gudrun gently stroked her hair, and said quietly to the weeping girl, "You are too young to know how a woman's heart clings to a man when they have exchanged kisses. I love Herwig, I am betrothed to Herwig, and I will be true to Herwig till I die."

Ortrun was dismayed, thinking she could never take her brother this news, and fearing that her mother would be angrier than ever with Gudrun.

So she reported as little of Gudrun's answer as she could, and managed things so cunningly that she was able to look after Gudrun herself for many weeks. Gudrun's poor hands grew as soft as ever, and color came back into her pale cheeks. But when Lord Hartmut spoke to her, she replied reluctantly, and glanced coldly at him, until

Hartmut's faint hopes died in spite of Ortrun's encouragement. He equipped himself for another, longer voyage, because he hated his own home now. He set out and Ortrun's bright eyes were red when he left; she knew it meant the return of loneliness, and winter, and their old way of life.

When Gerlind, watching from her window, saw the last gleam of weapons carried by Hartmut's men disappear, she went down and summoned Gudrun.

"We do not tame a wild colt with sugar," she said, "we tame it with whip and spurs! If your pride cannot be broken, grandchild of Hagen the Devil, then you shall do work for me now such as you never did before!"

"Lady, I will willingly do whatever you ask."

Gerlind spoke slowly, looking her in the face, a wolfish gleam in her own eyes. "You shall wash my clothes every day, and those of my household. And if I find you lazy in your work you shall feel the rod, as sure as my name is Gerlind!"

Just for a moment Gerlind thought Gudrun swayed on her feet, as if now, at last, she would burst into tears and beg for mercy and grovel to her. But Hagen's granddaughter closed her golden eyes, and when she opened them again Gudrun was smiling. "Then tell someone to teach me how to wash clothes, and do it today, for that was a lesson my mother never taught me. However, I am glad to know how to earn my living here, Lady Gerlind.

I should not like to be in your house without paying for my keep."

Gerlind sent for a washerwoman, who came in wooden clogs and a ragged dress, her hair tangled and her face and hands roughened by wind and salt water. She could not take her eyes off Gudrun as they went down to the shore, where she taught the princess how to wash the marks of rusty iron and sweat and blood off the warriors' clothes, kneeling on the sharp stones with the icy wind blowing around them and washing in the sea water, water as salty as tears.

When the other hostages heard of Gerlind's new act of cruelty, they felt that God and all living creatures had forgotten them. Many cursed the day they were born as women, wishing for a man's heart and a good sword to kill Lady Gerlind there in the castle courtyard itself, and to kill red-haired Heregart too: she had gone riding down to the shore with her handsome cupbearer, laughing, to watch Gudrun wash clothes.

When Gudrun came staggering home the first evening, so tired she felt she could have died, Hildburg of Frisia went to Lady Gerlind in private.

"God help us, you should not let Gudrun wash clothes alone! My father is a king too, like hers. Such work is not fit for us to do, but I should like to share whatever Gudrun suffers!"

Gerlind looked at Hildburg, who was small like her

own mother, Hildburg of Portugal, and slight and brown as a young deer.

"Impossible!" she said roughly. "It would be too much for you. Winter is coming and you would have to kneel on the snow in the icy wind. You would wish you were sitting in a warm room then, embroidering white robes with jewels!"

Hildburg's slender body quivered with anger and hatred and she cried, "Are you thoughtful on my account, when you have no pity for Gudrun? Whatever she suffers I will suffer too." And she ran to find Gudrun, laughing. "I have told that wicked she-wolf I will wash clothes with you!"

Gudrun put both arms around her and embraced her gently. "May Jesus Christ reward you for your goodness! The time will pass more quickly with two of us down on the shore."

So next morning both kings' daughters washed the Normans' dirty clothes, and nights and days came and went, came and went, until the seventh year after the great battle on the Wulpensand. . . .

But when seven years were up, Lord Frute came to Hilde's court. He had visited Matalane every year during all that long time, and every year she took him down to the harbor and asked anxiously if he thought they had enough ships and weapons yet. The blows of woodcutters' axes were ringing out in every forest of the Hegelings' land, and tree trunks, stripped of their bark and shining white, were sent rolling down every hillside, and every smith in the land was hammering away at red-hot iron. But each year Frute said nothing, and rode away.

Now it was Christmas and Frute came again. He saw a change in Hilde's face as she welcomed him. They rode down to the shore, and Lady Hilde watched in silence, smiling, as Lord Frute counted the ships which stretched far out into the harbor under the weak sun, side by side, mast by mast, sail close by sail. They were freshly painted in bright colors, and their standards were spotless white, blowing in the wind. Frute saw brown-skinned boys swarming up the new rigging like climbing beetles. One of them, whose hair was fair as flax, shouted down, laughing, "When are we off to visit the land of Normandy, sir?"

"Sooner than Lord Ludwig would like, I think," murmured Frute, and he straightened in his saddle.

They rode back to Matalane, and Lady Hilde had the armory opened with the key that never left her hands. Her own old menservants, who had come from Ireland with her, guarded the place. Hook after hook had been driven into the walls of the armory, and on each hook hung a mailshirt and a helmet, shining like silver. Below them shields leaned against the wall, sparkling in the light that fell in through the doorway. Great sheaves of spears stood upright in clusters, and new swords were heaped high on the floor, with only the narrowest of pathways left between them. Hilde's old servants stood ranked on these pathways, smiling broadly, and they asked, "When will the Normans get a sight of Hegeling weapons again, sir?"

"Sooner than Lady Gerlind dreams, I think," said Frute, and he too smiled as they left the armory.

Lady Hilde went on. They visited the stables, where Frute saw horse after horse, well-fed, their coats shining —heavy Danish warhorses whose dams he had known as foals, tough Arab horses, fiery Spanish horses of the kind that fight along with their riders, carrying long spikes on their chests to kill like their masters' swords.

Lady Hilde still went on. They looked at cattle whose large eyes gazed back at them, fat pigs surrounded by crowds of squealing piglets, an enormous fleecy flock of lambs marked with Hilde's red household sign.

They went into the storerooms and the smokehouse, with its tall roof, smelling of juniper and soot and pine needles, where the hams of wild boars and sides of bacon with a whitish crust on them were hanging. There were great crates of ship's biscuit, and big casks of wine, dried fish and huge cheeses the size of cartwheels. And finally Lady Hilde went into Matalane castle itself, leading Frute by the hand, and made him look down from the staircase into the courtyard below. Down there he heard the sound of a ball game, and cheerful laughter: there were troops of bright-eyed young men there, lively and light-footed. They were led by a youth who was not a boy any more, but not quite a fully grown man yet. He struck the ball fast and well, leaping confidently after it like a leopard, quite unaware of his own charm.

Then Frute laughed out loud, and Lord Ortwin looked up, shouted a glad welcome, and came leaping up the stairs.

"How like Gudrun he is!" said Frute.

Hilde took his arm and said, between hope and fear, "Do you still want more, Lord Frute?"

"The time has come!" he said. "Send out your messengers!"

So good men carried Hilde's standard out through all the countries. They came as far as the land of Alzabé, where they were given a great welcome, and when they left they took gifts of gold with them, and the long, curled feathers of a brightly colored bird as a token that the Prince of the Moors would keep his promise to Lady Hilde.

Armies came up from all the lands around like clouds scudding across the sky. Early spring was cold, the sea was stormy, the roads were soft and bad, but still they came in their thousands, and every pale ray of the sun was reflected in their weapons.

The army pitched camp outside Matalane. Tent stood

beside tent, the standards blowing above them in the March wind. A shield was planted in the ground outside the tent of each prince for every company of a hundred men that he had brought with him, and Frute counted many shields.

Lord Morung, who had the kidnapping of a child to avenge, like Lady Hilde, strode impatiently through the ranks. "I have been counting the shields too," he told Frute. "We have sixty thousand good men here! There is no need to wait for the Moors."

"We have waited seven years, Lord Morung, so now let us have all the strength we can. The lord of Alzabé said he would bring us twenty thousand warriors."

But Horand saw Lord Herwig let his breath out in a sigh of relief, as if he were not in such a hurry as Lord Morung for the army to set out.

That evening Herwig was sitting in the hall, one of the speckled hounds curled up asleep at his feet, when a man came up to him. He came silently, the floorboards did not creak, only the hound opened a watchful eye. Lord Horand sat down quietly on the end of the bench, and at once the dog got up, went over and laid his heavy head on Horand's knee. The brown eyes watched, unblinking, as the singer's gentle hand played with the hangings. A gray squirrel appeared and leaped up on Horand's shoulder. And finally the cat stalked over from the hearth.

"Send those creatures packing!" said Herwig, impatiently.

"Those in search of peace come to me," said Lord Horand, out of the shadows, and it seemed as if his voice had grown even sweeter since he gave up his singing.

"And did we not have peace here? Look: seven years have passed, and now they are setting out to rescue Gudrun. No one asks: what will she be like when we find her again? Who knows, a golden-eyed boy, Hartmut's heir, may welcome us to Normandy."

Horand said nothing for a while, and the dog sighed contentedly under the touch of his hand. Then the singer said, "Herwig, there may well be women who change, blowing out one torch and lighting another every day. But there are other, rarer women, whose love is like the fire that never goes out, burning before the cross forever . . ."

Lord Horand rose. The squirrel ran scuttling along the table, the hound followed Horand out of the hall: only the cat stayed and climbed gently onto Herwig's knee.

At last the ships from Alzabé arrived: very strange they looked—tall, with striped red and green silken awnings. The Prince of the Moors brought twenty thousand men armed with curved swords to join the Hegelings, and his brown face shone with joy between his dangling earrings. They began to get the weapons, provisions and horses on board ship. When the fleet was ready to set sail, Lady Hilde came down to thank them all for their loyalty. She brought out Hettel's white standard, stained brown with his blood, and unfurled it in front of them all; they lowered their swords at the sight of it. "You shall follow the standard bearer I name," said Hilde. "Any man who stands by him will not falter in the battle." And she went up to Horand of Denmark and offered him the old banner. He bowed one knee before her, took it and tied it to his spear shaft. Privately, Lady Hilde asked all her friends to look after her dear son Ortwin, and Wate swore by his own head that he would bring the young king home safe and sound. Ortwin himself was impatient to be off. He and his young companions had all been orphaned on the Wulpensand, and they were thirsty for blood and vengeance.

The sea was smooth, the wind was like a huge hand pushing the fleet gently forward over the shining surface of the water. Soon they reached the Wulpensand, where their fathers lay under the stone memorial. They went on land and kneeled before the graves, which were well tended by the white-robed monks. The Hegelings gave more money to build a monastery beside the little church and make the place a holy one.

When the others were going back to their ships, Wate went to Hettel's grave mound. He thrust the point of his drawn sword into the frozen earth with all his might, and as he leaned there on his sword he did not look down, he looked up at the sky where the clouds were driving.

"I have not forgotten, my king," he said. "I have not forgotten one word of my oath."

But when they sailed away from the Wulpensand it seemed as if their luck had turned. A storm got up, a treacherous March storm that blew them out to sea. The waves were black and boiling, the wind wailed in the rigging like a night bird screeching, it sighed in the sails, and the ships lay low in the water as if they carried some hidden cargo.

"It is the warriors from the Wulpensand, coming with us," said Frute, who saw more than other men. Wate was steering their ship, covered in spray from the breakers, and all the while sea birds circled above them under that gray, stormtorn sky, their shadows swooping overhead, dropping as if to attack, then rising with a flapping of their wings. Soon mist came up, wrapping them around like a damp and moldy shroud.

"The dead want something," said Frute, "but I cannot understand what it is."

Horand said, "I have been thinking: perhaps they are trying to warn us against committing new wrongs when we have set out to avenge old wrongs done to us. We must not be harsher to the land of Normandy than Christian knights should be."

As soon as he had said that, the mist parted like a dark

sheet torn apart, and suddenly the ship beneath their feet rose higher in the water, shuddering.

"Land ahead!" cried the lookouts.

"It is the coast of Normandy!" said Lord Horand. He knew a bay surrounded by woods where the ships could not be seen from the castle towers, so they anchored there.

Tired after their voyage, the men camped under ancient pine trees with branches so thick they made a roof which the snow could hardly penetrate. The Hegelings were glad to feel the firm ground, covered with pine needles, and it was good to drink from a spring, still surrounded by ice, and pick wrinkled berries from the bushes. But Frute would not let them rest for long; they were near the enemy now. He made them bring the horses on land. They were stiff from standing on the ships, and Frute had them given double rations of oats to prepare them for the next day's fighting.

"And test every collar and girth today," he said. "A man's life may depend on it. Anyone who does not think his mailshirt is good enough may exchange it for a better one. Lady Hilde gave us five hundred sets of mail and weapons when we left, beside our own."

They lit fires and brought food from the ships, cutting into wild boar hams with their knives while the horses pushed their noses into shields heaped high with oats. Frute knew that the time to feed horses and men is the night before a battle, not in the morning. The warriors were well fed and tired, and sleep soon overcame them. Fire after fire burned down, casting a glowing rosy light on the reddish pine trunks, which seemed to stretch on forever in the dark, and on the helmets of the sentries circling around the camp.

Still awake, Wate and Frute sat beside one of the fires; they were too old to need much sleep. Herwig was with them, his chin propped on both hands, staring into the crackling flames, and Horand, who sometimes ran his hand over his sword blade, listening to the note it sounded. This had become a habit of his since he had sworn his oath and left his songs to wither unsung.

Ortwin lay asleep at their feet, under the cloak Wate had spread over him. All that could be seen of him was his bright golden head and his closed eyes.

Wate looked up at the black and starless sky.

"One more day to dawn," he said, "and then no Norman will be able to say the king of the Hegelings lies in his grave unavenged!"

But Lord Frute, whispering as if he were putting his most secret thoughts into words, said, "We ought to send out a spy first. We cannot attack both castles at once without knowing if they are likely to come upon us from behind."

Wate laughed. "There's one good thing about *that* suggestion—any man who goes out spying needn't worry about finding his way back. Ludwig's men will certainly catch him and hang him."

"All the same," replied Frute, "we must send spies before we attack. We need to know where they keep the women. Otherwise they could have them hidden where we shall not find them easily."

The Prince of the Moors laughed, with a flash of his white teeth. "A sword is the best key to all doors. And we have eighty thousand such keys hanging at our belts!"

"Whom would you send to Karadein?" Horand asked Frute quietly.

"Send me!" cried Ortwin suddenly, laughing, flinging back Wate's cloak, and leaping up from the ground, fresh and warm from sleep.

"Do you want to be the death of me?" thundered Wate. "Have you forgotten I swore by my own head to protect you?"

"If you will go spying out the land, Ortwin, I will come with you," said Herwig, rising to his full slender height. He spoke slowly but very firmly. "No one can deny that Ortwin has a right to go looking for his sister, and I have a right to go in search of my betrothed wife."

Then there was much talk and argument, but Frute agreed with them. However, he advised them to wait for daylight before setting out, because it was a long way to row to the castles, close as they might seem. So the heroes sat in silence around the fire till the pale light of dawn. And Herwig thought no night in all his life had ever been so long. The next day would bring him either within sight of Gudrun again, or to the bitter death of a spy.

CHAPTER SEVEN

How the swan spoke in a human voice
The washerwomen on the shore
How two fishermen came
How Gudrun threw Gerlind's clothes into the sea

It was a misty morning in the season of Lent, and Gudrun and Hildburg stood on the seashore washing clothes as they did every day. The wind blew in icy squalls, whipping their wet skirts around them as they wrung out the heavy cloaks, which formed heavy coils like great snakes. Hildburg could hardly stand upright. She had been miserably ill for days now, but hard as Gudrun begged her she said she would never ask Lady Gerlind to let her stay in the castle and rest.

As long as Gerlind's woodcutters and huntsmen were passing through the woods, the girls laughed and sang at their work, so that news of their proud courage would be taken back to the wicked queen. Later on no one came near them but the crows, cawing hungrily in the trees, and once a red vixen passed with her three sharpnosed cubs: they were kinder than Gerlind and took no pleasure in the girls' tears.

Even the vixen had gone now and the kings' daughters were all alone. The sky was gloomy and gray, and the forest behind them was black. The sun sank lower and lower and they still had piles of clothes to wash.

Then Hildburg began to moan, quietly; there was no sound but her quiet weeping and the roar of the sea breaking on the shore, gray and pitiless as ever, its waves trickling back again through the pebbles shifting in the water.

Gudrun went on washing as if she had not heard anything. But though Horand had taught her well, telling her to remember both in joy and sorrow that all things pass, she thought her heart could not bear it much longer: the waves forever coming in, the wind chilling her to the bone, Hildburg's quiet tears while she herself must be strong.

And in our blindness, we know so little of what Fate has in store that Gudrun's courage at last began to fail her at the very moment when the Hegelings set foot on Norman soil.

As Hildburg huddled there, sobbing, and Gudrun wrung out a heavy cloak of Hartmut's with her frozen hands, the swirling mist before them suddenly parted, as if a sword had cut it through. A great white bird came swimming toward them on the twilit sea, gliding soundlessly, its neck gracefully arched. It came closer and closer, like a silvery shimmer of light.

"You lovely swan!" said Gudrun. "How sorry I am for you! Are you homeless too, swimming here on the cold sea so late in the day?"

She stepped gently down to the water and, since the bird stayed still, looking at her with wise, yellow eyes, she leaned forward to stroke its smooth wings, which were the color of newly fallen snow. But she snatched her hand back when the bird spoke—spoke out loud in a human voice.

"I am a messenger from God to you, Gudrun! Your sufferings here are over. Ask me what you like, noble lady, and I will answer you!"

Gudrun ran back to Hildburg, and the two of them pressed close together, unable to believe their ears when they heard a wild swan speak in human language. They glanced around them, and back into the woods, thinking someone was playing a heartless trick. But there was no one else on the bleak seashore, only the two girls and the white bird, which shone like the reflection of invisible stars. Gudrun fell on her knees, opening wide her arms to the swan.

"If Christ himself has sent you, dear messenger of God, then tell me in his name, is my mother Hilde still alive?"

Rocking up and down on the water, which was black, the bird said, "I saw your mother Hilde alive and well as I flew over Matalane. And she has gathered such an army as no woman ever gathered before to come and rescue you."

The poor washerwoman clasped her hands and allowed her tears to fall. "Tell me, dear messenger of God, is my young brother Ortwin still alive?"

Rocking on the water, which was crystal clear, the beautiful bird said, "Ortwin is a grown man now, and he is bringing Hettel's sword to his first battle, where he will soon show his courage!"

Gudrun cried out for joy, her cheeks flaming. "Oh, tell me, dear messenger of God!" she said. "Is my beloved Herwig, my betrothed husband, still alive?"

Then the water where the swan was rocking became a stream of molten gold, and the swan said joyfully, "Yes, indeed, Lord Herwig of Zealand is alive!"

Then it spread its wings and rose from the waves in a shower of gold.

Gudrun hurried toward it on her knees, over the wet

pebbles, reaching out her hands. "For Our Lord's sake, I beg you to tell me how much longer we must wait? Will Hildburg see her home again? Are Wate and Frute alive? They were not young when last I saw them."

By now the bird was only a swirl of mist in the gathering dusk, but its light still lingered on the water. "If you call on me in Our Lord's name, I must answer. Be steadfast: there is not long to wait. Tomorrow you will see two more messengers, dearer to you than I am!"

With these words, the swan flew away. Night was all around them, but one star shone with a comforting light in the cold winter sky.

They went home, their hearts in turmoil, joyful and yet uncertain. Gerlind spoke harshly to them, saying they had been idle and worked badly that day. All they had to eat was hard rye bread, with a little water to help it down, and the longer they talked the more the two poor girls felt they had been dreaming.

They lay down to sleep on their hard benches. Hildburg coughed and coughed, shivering without any pillow or blankets; Gerlind had taken those away long ago.

They woke early in the morning, stiff with cold, as the first light of day came in through the narrow window. Hildburg forced herself to get up and see what the weather was like. When she saw great snowflakes falling from the sky the poor girl pressed her hand to her hot, feverish forehead, weeping bitterly.

"If God does not help us, and I have to wash clothes standing barefoot on the ice all day, they will find me dead on the stony shore!"

Gudrun stroked her curly dark hair and comforted her. "Dearest, let us go to that she-wolf Gerlind," she said. "Perhaps she will give us shoes and warmer clothes!"

They went on tiptoe through the corridors of the sleeping castle, and Hildburg pressed her hands to her mouth to keep from coughing. They stood outside Gerlind's bedchamber door for a long time, listening to Lord Ludwig's regular breathing. At last Gudrun opened the door. Lady Gerlind lay there, with Ludwig's gray head resting peacefully on her arm. The pair of them slept softly, among blankets and white furs, and there was a fire crackling on the hearth.

Hildburg's quiet weeping woke Gerlind. Once roused from sleep, she asked angrily, "What are you doing here? You should have been down on the shore washing clothes by now!"

"I doubt if we can wash clothes today," said Gudrun. "The snow has been falling all night and Hildburg is hot with fever."

"You shall wash my clothes whether you like it or not! It was your own choice and I warned you myself, Hildburg! Palm Sunday is coming, and if our men do not have white robes to wear to church service, you'll be sorry for it!" Another fit of coughing shook Hildburg, and wicked Gerlind shouted, so loud that it roused Ludwig, "Why should I care if I saw the pair of you lying dead?"

She jumped out of bed and flung a huge bundle wrapped in a cloth at Gudrun's feet.

Using all her strength, Gudrun picked up the bundle by its knot. She looked at the queen's malicious face, and said quietly, "God will repay you for this, Lady Gerlind!" Then she carried the bundle all by herself, supporting Hildburg at the same time, as they walked barefoot through the snow in the castle courtyard.

But the washerwoman who had first taught Gudrun to wash clothes came shuffling through the snow after them. She gave Hildburg her own wooden shoes, and her own red shawl, and made each of them drink a mug of hot goat's milk; people who have suffered themselves know what suffering is like.

And she took the bundle of clothes from Gudrun and carried it down to the shore on her own broad shoulders.

The two kings' daughters stood there as they did every day, washing clothes for Hartmut's warriors. Hildburg could not work fast, because her chest hurt and icy chills and waves of heat ran through her limbs. But Gudrun's hands flew, and she kept looking around and out to sea, to where she had seen the bird come swimming to make them promises.

However, the feeble wintry sun rose higher in the sky, and began to sink again, and still no one came. Wet snow and icy rain fell, and the wind blew at the cloaks they were washing till they billowed out like sails. Their fingers were numb and frozen. The early twilight of a winter's day came on, and Hildburg's hands faltered and stopped more and more often. As for Gudrun, her head was not raised now, but bowed hopelessly over the linen she was washing.

And then Hildburg saw a tiny boat coming toward them, rowed by two fishermen in brown hooded cloaks. She said, timidly, "Look—look there! Do you think these are your messengers, Gudrun?"

Gudrun rose from her knees. She looked at the boat, then she looked down at herself, and a flush of shame rose in her pale cheeks. "If God is good, and these are really messengers from my mother, I am glad and sorry both at once for them to find me here! Suppose they tell my mother they saw me washing clothes on the shore! How could she bear it?" She took Hildburg's hand in both of hers. "Oh, dearest, tell me what to do! Shall we run away, when maybe we could help our rescuers? Shall we stay and let my mother's men see our shame?"

"Do not ask me for advice!" said gentle Hildburg. "Whatever you do, I will do the same. I will stay with you whatever happens!"

The fishermen's strong arms were rowing the little boat closer and closer; they were waving now and calling out. Gudrun suddenly seized Hildburg's hand and they ran across the frozen sand toward the forest. The two fishermen saw them. They jumped out of their boat, and the taller man shouted out loud, "Why are you in such a hurry, pretty washerwomen? We're strangers; you ought not to trust us! If you leave the clothes here you might well lose them!"

When Gudrun heard his voice all her blood shot to her heart; she clutched at it with her hand, as if otherwise it would break. Her knees were weak beneath her, but when she turned to see the face under the hood she felt it was strange to her. As for Herwig, King of Zealand, who had no idea how close he was to his beloved Gudrun, he called out again, "Come back, you pretty girls, in the name of all virtuous maidens! We shall not hurt you."

Gudrun took a step toward him, saying quietly, "If you ask in the name of all virtuous maidens, I cannot honorably refuse to come."

And the two girls went back to the water's edge, their wet shifts clinging to them and making them shiver in the cold as they walked. They wore kerchiefs on their heads, but the March wind had torn locks of hair free, and they hung over the girls' foreheads and cheeks, wet with snow. The two men thought that their limbs shone whiter in the dusk than the snow beneath their feet. King Herwig bowed, and spoke courteously to them both, not in the way a fisherman would usually address washerwomen. The two princesses found that sweet; their wicked mistress seldom so much as wished them good morning or good evening.

"Now, give us news!" said young Ortwin, and Gudrun's heart suddenly sank. She thought that if the other man was really her beloved Herwig, then Horand or another of his faithful friends would have come with him, not a stranger whose voice she did not recognize. "Who is it who makes you wash clothes here, when you are both so beautiful, and you seem to be of noble birth? Does your master have more washerwomen as lovely as you?"

"Many far more lovely than myself," said Gudrun sadly, and now she thought the men's faces under their hoods were quite strange to her. "Ask what you want to know and ask quickly. I think I see a woodcutter walking through the forest, and if he tells our mistress we spoke to you, she will make us pay dearly for it."

"Do not be afraid!" said Herwig. "Here, take our payment! We will give you these four bracelets if you tell us what we want to know."

"Keep your good gold; we shall not take any payment," said Gudrun quietly, and once again she felt she was hearing Herwig's own voice.

"Then accept our thanks and tell us who owns those tall castles we see over there?"

"One belongs to Lord Ludwig, the other to Lord Hartmut, and the land of Normandy belongs to the two of them."

"We should like to meet those kings!" said Lord Ortwin. "Can you tell us whether they are at home, and if they have warriors with them?"

Gudrun answered quickly and joyfully. "I saw King Ludwig asleep in his bed this very morning, and he has some ten thousand men with him."

"And do you know, beautiful washerwoman," asked Herwig, "why Ludwig keeps such a strong force in his castle when his country is at peace?"

Gudrun came closer, and in the dusk of the snowy March evening her burning eyes stared at his face in the shadow of his hood. "Yes, I know why Ludwig hides behind so many shields! He is afraid of a people called the Hegelings."

The Prince of Zealand saw that the poor washerwoman was trembling all over, and he thought it was from cold. He took off his fisherman's cloak and was going to put it around her, but she looked straight at him and said, very softly, "God reward you for your kindness, but I will never wear a man's clothes!"

They looked at one another, and in the twilight it seemed to Herwig as if she were very like the girl he longed for. He sighed deeply.

"Since you mention the Hegelings," said Ortwin, "no doubt you know that a king's daughter once came here from their country, with her ladies."

Then Herwig leaped forward, crying, "Ortwin, if your sister is still alive at all, here she is! No two women could be so alike!"

When Gudrun heard Ortwin's name, and Herwig's warm hand grasped hers, she felt she would die of joy. But her heart warned her to test Herwig's love and see if it had changed, or if it was strong enough to forget how low she had been brought. She gently withdrew her hand. "If you are looking for Gudrun, do not search among the living," she said. "The Princess of the Hegelings died of grief long ago."

Herwig's arms fell to his sides, and he swayed on his feet like a man pierced to the heart by an arrow. Ortwin turned aside in silence to hide the tears rising to his eyes.

Her voice wavering, Gudrun said, "Are you so sorry to hear that, my lords? Was the lady one of your family?"

She took no notice of Hildburg, who was pulling her by the sleeve and making signs to her. Then Herwig threw back his head and flung out his arms; the mailshirt he was wearing under his fisherman's clothes clashed. "Yes, indeed I am sorry for Gudrun's death. I shall mourn her all my life. If only I had taken her away as my wife when we were solemnly betrothed! Now Ludwig's treachery has lost me my happiness forever!"

Gudrun put out her hand to him and said, through her tears, "Herwig, do you know this ring?" And dark as it was, Herwig knew it at once. It was the stone from Araby his mother had once worn. He took Gudrun in his arms and kissed her, and stopped to look at her, and then kissed her again and again, and he kissed Hildburg too. Hildburg began to feel that happiness is the best medicine in the world.

But when they had all finished laughing and weeping in their amazement and delight, Ortwin asked jokingly the thing Herwig had feared in earnest—the thought that had haunted his lonely nights. "Well, sister, and why does Lord Hartmut let you wash clothes here when you are the mother of his children?"

Gudrun looked straight at him with her golden eyes. "How could I have children? All the people of Normandy know I am washing clothes here on the shore because I would have nothing to do with Hartmut's love, or wear his crown!"

At that Herwig let out a great laugh like a drunken man. He seized Gudrun, lifted her and wrapped her tightly in his brown cloak. Covering her face with kisses, he carried her across the icy sand and into the cold waves. He had almost reached the little boat when Ortwin cried, "Herwig, where are you taking her?" Herwig turned, one foot already in the boat. "I am not leaving her under Hartmut's roof one night longer!"

"No, stop!" cried Ortwin. "Did we come to steal women ourselves? If I had a hundred sisters, I would not let anyone say of me that I came like a thief on my first campaign to steal back what the Normans took in open battle!"

Reluctantly, Herwig stepped back from the boat, but he clasped Gudrun even closer to his heart. "Ortwin, I am afraid that once they see our army they will hide the girls where we shall never find them again," he said.

"So you want to rescue Gudrun, thinking of no one but yourself, and abandon the other noble ladies? You may cut me in pieces before I agree to any such thing!"

Then Herwig began wading back through the cold waves, over the icy sand, and Gudrun's arms wound around his neck in terror, as if she would never let him go. "What is to become of me?" she cried; it was as if she lost all her proud strength now that help had come. "Ortwin, what have I ever done to hurt you, my brother? Why are you doing this to me now?"

Ortwin kissed her mouth, saying, "Trust me, Gudrun. I do not want to hurt you, but I must take you away from here honorably, like a good knight!" He leaped into the boat and took the tiller. "Herwig! We must go!" he cried.

At last Herwig tore himself away. Gudrun fell to her knees. "I was the happiest of women, and now I am unhappy again! What comfort can you give me, Herwig?"

Herwig called back, kissing his hand to her. "You are

always the lady of my heart! Before the sun rises tomorrow, I shall be back with eighty thousand men. I shall be as true to you as you have been to me!"

Hildburg helped Gudrun up from her knees, and they waved to the boat that carried all their hopes as long as they could see so much as its shadowy outline in the dark.

On hearing that eighty thousand men were there to rescue her, only waiting for morning, all Gudrun's fear and grief left her. But Hildburg was still afraid to go back to the castle that evening, because of Gerlind. She asked Gudrun to help her finish their work; there were still a great many cloaks to wash.

Gudrun raised her head and laughed, with her lips closed. "Two kings have kissed me today. My heart is too proud to wash that she-wolf's clothes now!"

Hildburg warned her anxiously, "Gerlind can still do us harm before morning."

Gudrun's eyes blazed. "If she were to beat me with birch twigs all night, I would not die! Now see how I wash Gerlind's clothes for her!"

And she began throwing the cloaks out into the sea, with both hands. They floated there, billowing out. Hildburg pleaded with her to stop, but Gudrun only laughed. It was dark night when they came home, and Hildburg, stumbling, carried the things they had already washed, but Hettel's daughter walked free and empty-handed. Gerlind was standing at the castle gate. When she saw the two royal washerwomen come back so late, her rage boiled over.

"Who said you might stay out so long? You are not worthy to serve a noble queen even as washerwomen!" She went up to Gudrun, fists clenched, raging at Gudrun's smile, and hissed into her face, "Laugh, would you? Do you think it does you any credit to refuse a great king's crown, and then stand gossiping on the beach at night with common fishermen?"

"You are lying, Lady Gerlind. I have never gossiped with common fishermen in my life!"

"You wicked girl!" cried the queen. "You dare to say I'm lying? My own servants saw you down on the beach —and I shall beat you for it tonight!"

"I should not advise you to do that," said Gudrun, smiling. "I am of nobler blood than any of your family!"

And only now did Gerlind, who had been blind with rage, see that Gudrun had no bundle with her.

"Have you come back empty-handed?" she screamed. "Where have you left all my good clothes?"

"Down by the sea, but I do not know whether they are still there, and I do not care much if you get them back again. They were too heavy for me." And secretly she stroked Hildburg's hand to comfort her, because Hildburg was weeping quietly for fear of what would happen now.

"I will pay you back for that, this very evening!" said Gerlind.

She called loudly for her own women, and made them bind twigs into birches. When the Hegeling hostages heard how Gudrun was to be punished they all came and fell at wicked Gerlind's feet, begging her to have mercy. But all the time red-haired Heregart stood in the doorway, wearing rich robes, and nibbling the sweet cake she was holding, indifferent to Gudrun's fate.

Gerlind told Gudrun and Hildburg to follow her to her own bedchamber, and she locked the door herself. She told Gudrun of the Hegelings and Hildburg of Frisia to take off their wet shifts; she tied them to the bedstead with new willow withes. But when she picked up her birch, raising it for the first stroke, Hagen the Wild's granddaughter looked at her. "Do you think you are doing your son much honor, Lady Gerlind," she asked, "if people may point at me and say his mother beat me?" Gerlind and Hildburg both stared at her as she went on. "Because I have changed my mind, Lady Gerlind. I wish to rule the kingdom of Normandy now—and believe me, I speak the truth!"

The birch fell from Gerlind's hands and she clapped them together. She began to laugh so happily that all the ill temper vanished from her face—for she did not see any double meaning in what Gudrun said. "Praise be to God, my son will be happy at last!" she cried, quickly bending to untie Gudrun and Hildburg.

"Our sufferings are over now," said Gudrun, "and you ought to look after us well. Send someone to tell Lord Hartmut what I have said."

One of Gerlind's pages heard her, out in the hall, and he ran to Hartmut's own castle as fast as his slender legs would carry him. He burst into the hall where Hartmut was sitting with his men. His face was as red as a poppy and he was quite breathless as he knelt.

"Give me a messenger's reward for good news, my lord! Gudrun the golden has changed her mind!"

Hartmut sprang up from the chessboard, and the ivory pieces fell and broke on the floor. "If your news were true I would give you rich acres of land and sixty golden bracelets!"

Lady Gerlind's own chamberlain came up, panting, and knelt beside the nimble page. "Let us share the reward then, my lord! Lady Gerlind sent *me* to you with this good news!"

Hartmut laughed out loud, and gave both of them the full reward, and more than he had promised. As for the count who had been playing chess with him, he gave him the golden chessboard as a memento.

He hurried to Gerlind's own apartments. There stood Gudrun, smiling her strange and magical smile at him, her brows raised. Hartmut reached out his arms to her, longing to kiss her soft mouth at long, long last. But Gudrun refused him, though in a softer voice than any he had heard her use. "No, sir, not yet. It would do you no honor! I am a poor washerwoman and you are a great king; it would not be right for you to hold me in your arms. Let my women see to me tonight, and tomorrow I will show you what is in my heart!"

"I will always do whatever you like," said Lord Hartmut quietly.

"Then let them call for my ladies! I have not had them near me for many years. And have them well cared for too, according to their rank and noble blood. Their grief has been as great as their loyalty to me."

She smiled at Hartmut, and he went away with his mind in a turmoil, intoxicated by his love for her. He gave orders to the Normans to set free the hostages and look after them all well, with baths, and good food, and rich clothes. He had a banquet fit for a king prepared for them. Doors opened in the castle of Karadein, and out poured the Hegeling women. They were shabbily dressed, and their hair was unadorned; wicked Gerlind had made them work their hands to the bone all these years. But when they had bathed and dressed, they were lovely as stars in the sky, while Gudrun was the golden sun.

The feast was brought in and there was good wine to drink. Gerlind's own cupbearer poured the wine for them, and so red-haired Heregart came into the hall with him, an uncertain smile on her lips. She sat down at the table, talked a great deal and laughed loudly, although none of Gudrun's ladies answered her. It was like talking to the empty air, and at last she fell silent. But when the pages brought in the second course, another girl came up to Gudrun. She was as lovely as a May morning: it was Ortrun, who had come with her own women to kiss her new sister.

"How glad I am to see the day when you are betrothed to my brother!" cried Ortrun. "Gudrun, I shall give you my mother's circlet with the green stones, which was meant for my own betrothal day!"

Gudrun rose and looked at her earnestly. "May God reward you for your good will, Ortrun! I shall repay you fully when all is well for me again!"

They drank their wine in small sips, but it brought a flush to their cheeks quickly. "Now you must say goodnight, dear daughters," said Lady Gerlind. "There are many happy days to come when you can sit together and talk as friends!"

Ortrun bowed obediently, but Gudrun took her in her arms and tenderly kissed her pretty face before she left the hall with her own ladies.

The stewards and chamberlains hurried to carry out the tables and bring in beds where Gudrun and her ladies could spend the night in the comfort suitable for a queen and her companions.

But just as they were about to lie down and rest on the furs and soft silks they had not known for years, one of the girls said, in a low, sad voice, "We shall never see our home again now. We shall stay in Normandy forever, though we came here against our own will!"

Seeing them all weeping, Gudrun grasped the two arms of her chair with both hands and, leaning back, she laughed her clear ringing laughter, which they had not heard for seven years. Then Heregart and Gerlind went pale, exchanging glances, and each of them felt chilled to the heart. Gerlind snatched up her cloak and ran across the snow in the dark, leaning into the wind, over to her son's castle of Kassiane.

Hartmut was lying on his bed, unable to sleep for happiness. She came and sat on the edge of the bed.

"What is the matter, Mother? You look as pale as if you had seen some terrible thing!"

"Hartmut, Gudrun laughed today, for the first time in seven years, for the first time on Norman soil. And when she laughed my heart froze. I thought I heard the clash of swords."

Hartmut put his arm round his mother, smiling. "You took no notice of her tears, Mother—are you afraid of her laughter now? I only wish I had been there myself! Gudrun is most beautiful of all when she laughs—as I remember!"

Lady Gerlind's hands worked impatiently. "Listen to

me!" she begged him. "This evening my servants saw two strange fishermen on the beach. They called out to the girls and then talked to them. Hartmut—suppose they were messengers from Hilde?"

"Are you afraid of the Hegelings, Mother? Never fear, they're at home in their warm beds snoring like the Seven Sleepers! Be happy, Mother, as happy as I am now that Gudrun is to be mine at last!"

So Lady Gerlind went back through the night, but her heart had never been so heavy.

When the chamberlains and pages had left, Gudrun said out loud, "Now, Lady Hildburg, close the doors, as you always used to do for us!"

The red-haired Duchess Heregart was standing in the doorway; she went red and then white, and did not know whether to go or stay. Her own task, in the old days, had been to undo Gudrun's plaits for the night, and her place had been on Gudrun's left hand, just as Hildburg's place had been on Gudrun's right. Hildburg hesitated at the door, not knowing what to do.

"All those who were not loyal shall be shut out now," said Gudrun quietly.

Proud Heregart bowed her head, and went away, and Hildburg was the only one who saw that she was weeping. Then Hildburg shot four bolts across the oaken doors, and Gudrun made sure they were well fastened, so that no sound could be heard outside. Then she went up to her women and held out her hands to them. "You have shed many tears, but now is the time to laugh instead! This very day Hildburg and I kissed Ortwin and my beloved Herwig. All our sorrows are over now. They are coming back tomorrow to set us free, with eighty thousand men! And I will give a strong castle as dowry to whoever wakes me before sunrise. I mean to sleep well and soundly tonight, for the first time in seven long years."

CHAPTER EIGHT

How the count's daughter saw the Hegeling standards
Herwig saves Hartmut's life
Wate climbs the tower stairs
The voyage home
The four brides
How Horand sang the Saracen woman's song for the last time
The leave-taking

There was one of the Hegeling women who had been carried off to Normandy very young; even now she was only just sixteen. She was a lively girl, as those with fine skin, freckles and curly hair tend to be, and she was the one who slipped out of bed before anyone else was awake.

She was only a poor count's daughter, and she hoped to earn herself Gudrun's castle for a dowry. Blinking the sleep from her eyes and shivering, she looked out at the sky, where a narrow streak of rosy light was just beginning to show. Then she looked down at the twilit land around the castle and she nearly cried out loud. Horse beside horse, spear beside spear, as far as the eye could see, the Hegelings surrounded the castle of Karadein like a vast wall. Their army stretched far back into the misty countryside. She leaned forward and gazed further, all around the place: everywhere she looked the first light of dawn was reflected in the new helmets and spears of the motionless men. Their standards blew out in a fresh spring wind, and though the count's daughter had been a mere child when she last saw the Hegeling banners, she had not forgotten the colors under which her own people fought.

Restraining her impulse to cry out, and blinded by the sight, she hurried back into the room and knelt by Gudrun's bed weeping and laughing both at once, all thought of the castle forgotten in the joy that almost broke her heart. "Wake up, Lady Gudrun! God is good! Our friends have not forgotten us after all!"

Gudrun leaped out of bed and ran barefoot to the window. She too saw the wall of metal around the castle and the rosy light of dawn on the weapons. And Gudrun thought how soon they would be tinged red with blood.

"Alas!" she said, grief-stricken. "I am afraid to think how many noble men will die today!"

Just as she said this, a cry rang out from the tower above her: King Ludwig's sentry, shouting, "To arms, my lord, to arms! Wake, wake, you warriors! Get yourselves armed, you have slept too long! To arms, to arms, to arms!"

Gerlind heard him as she slept restlessly beside Lord Ludwig. She cast one glance down from her window and then ran back to the king, her hair flying loose. He was still lost in his dreams, so she shook him with all her might. "Wake up, Lord Ludwig! Our enemies are upon us! Your men will pay dearly for Gudrun's laughter today!"

"Let me see for myself," cried the king, fuddled with sleep and staggering to the window. As he looked down, Lord Horand was tying Hettel's bloodstained standard to the shaft of his spear. At that same moment the sun came fully up and shone into the king's dazzled eyes.

Lord Ludwig laughed. "Those are pilgrims—don't you see the sign of the cross on their banner? They are welcome to shelter here." And he slipped back into his warm bed, refusing to listen to Gerlind.

Then there was a clashing sound in the corridor outside, and the door was flung open. There stood Lord Hartmut, fully armed and very pale, like a man who has just buried his sweetest dream. "Do not let it alarm you too much,

Father and Mother," he said in a steady voice, "but down there I have counted the banners of thirty-three countries! I feel as if all the world has risen in arms to avenge Gudrun. And the man with the blood-stained banner at the head of them is Horand, Lady Hilde's standard bearer!"

The silence of Lord Ludwig's castle of Karadein suddenly turned to noise and haste. Men ran back and forth, rubbing sleep from their eyes, cursing and shouting for their armor. One man found that rats had nibbled through the straps of his shield, another found a nest of mice, a scrabbling heap of naked little pink and gray creatures, inside his helmet, a third could not draw his sword from its sheath for rust.

Women sobbed as their men pushed them aside, shouting at them, children clung to their mothers' skirts and screamed, horses neighed and stamped, voices shouted orders down into the courtyard, and everywhere there was the sound of clanging metal.

Hartmut's own men were ready waiting in the courtyard, their horses drawn up side by side, their armor shining and spotless. At their head their master, pale and drawn, held his naked sword in his hands. "Open the gate!" he said, rising in his stirrups. "If we are the only Normans to meet the Hegelings outside these castle walls, then the fame will all be ours!"

But when the porter put his hand to the bolts, Lady Gerlind ran in front of Hartmut's horse. She was still in her shift, just as she had jumped out of bed, though she had thrown a red shawl around her and was holding it together over her breast with her left hand, while she caught Hartmut's bridle with her right.

"What are you doing, Hartmut?" she cried, hoarse with terror. "Do you want to throw your own life away? My child, if you leave the castle the men out there will kill you! I know it!"

Hartmut bent down and gently loosened his mother's hands.

"Go indoors, Mother. Set your women to their own work, and leave us men to ours. The day has come for us to reap the harvest of your treatment of Gudrun."

Half mad with grief to think that she herself would have caused her son's death, Gerlind stammered, "I only wanted to help you. I thought I could break her will! It was all for your sake. Hartmut, take my advice just once more. The castles are strong; have their gates barricaded! Your enemies are ten to one against you outside, but we have provisions for a whole year in here. Tell your men to shoot arrows from the windows, leave your Hegelings to their own devices out there and pick them off gradually, but do not go out to them. Hartmut, *do not go out*! I will carry stones up to the battlements in my own cloak and throw them down on the Hegelings' heads!"

"Mother," said Hartmut, and though his voice was still gentle, a cold fire burned in his eyes. "I would rather have the ravens eat my corpse than let my enemies find me locked inside this castle. Follow me, men of Normandy! If it is God's will for us to come back, I shall reward you richly. And do not think, in the heat of battle, of your children who may be left orphans; I will care for them as if they were my own!"

He gave the signal, and Gerlind saw the great gates swing open as Hartmut's warriors stormed out of the castle.

It was the first time anyone had ever seen that proud, hard woman shed tears. She wept bitterly, standing there with a red shawl over her shift.

Wate was beside the standard on his dapple gray, his hand in its mailed glove shading his eyes as he looked around and saw the gates open. And when the riders came storming out of the gateway, Lord Wate raised his horn and took a deep breath. When he blew that horn, the sound could be heard a good three miles away. And when the Hegelings heard the horn call, they settled their helmets on their heads and raised their shields on their arms.

Wate blew for the second time, and the call of his horn could be heard a good ten miles away; his great warhorn was made of the horn of a gigantic animal, and he could draw a mighty sound from it. Then every man of the Hegelings drew his sword.

Wate blew his horn for the third time, his face red

beneath his gray beard, and thirty miles off a rock broke away from a stony cliff as if there were a great storm and fell splashing into the sea. Once the third horn call had rung out, Horand let the banner fly out free, and they could all see the stains of Hettel's blood.

There was silence over all the plain, and then Herwig gave an exultant shout—the signal to attack. The Hegelings rode forward over the frozen fields, the brightness of their spear points reflected in their enemies' eyes. Ortwin felt he could not restrain himself any longer, and he rose in his stirrups as he carried the banner of Ortland forward in his first battle.

Lady Gerlind stood on the battlements of Lord Ludwig's castle, leaning on Ortrun, her burning eyes watching the first clash of spears and swords.

When she saw the fighting begin, and the forest of waving banners, Ortrun started to cry quietly. Then she resolutely wiped away her tears, so as to see better. She turned to the red-haired Duchess Heregart, who was watching the familiar banners too, with her heart torn both ways at once, and asked who the young knight in white was.

"The hawk on the white ground is the banner of Ortland, so the man carrying it must be Lord Ortwin. I held him in my arms as a baby when I was only a child myself. But alas!—the man beside him is Lord Wate of Sturmen, and his anger is terrible when he is roused!"

Lady Gerlind began to groan and wail, seeing her son Hartmut fling himself into the thick of the fight. And he fought well, like a true king; no enemy could have denied it. Gerlind laughed triumphantly each time his sword blade went home, and then trembled and called down blessings on him and muttered charms.

When Ortwin saw the king fighting he asked Wate who it was striking such blows. Wate told him Hartmut's name, and Ortwin cried, "So that is Lord Hartmut, son of Ludwig who murdered my dear father! He shall pay for Hettel's death!"

Hearing him, Hartmut spurred on his horse, which soon carried him to Ortwin, and they charged at each other with their spears couched. They met with such force that Ortwin's white horse was thrown back on its haunches and Hartmut's own mount stumbled.

They leaped out of their saddles and their followers began to fight each other, too. The battle was like a whirlpool at this spot. Hartmut had fought like an honorable knight on many campaigns, and he did not intend to kill Ortwin, but Ortwin himself fought so bravely that Hartmut soon saw he would have hard work to defend himself.

Hartmut's blows began to rain down on Ortwin like a shower of hail, and Ortwin, so much younger, found it difficult to withstand them. When Wate saw Ortwin in danger he spurred his horse on and cut his way through the battle to his young master. However, before he could reach Ortwin to get his own shield in between him and Hartmut, Hartmut struck so hard that Ortwin's helmet was cut in two and flew to the ground. A trickle of red blood from a head wound ran down over his armor. Wate caught him up as he fell, flinging him over his shoulder as a huntsman does a deer, and carried him out of the battle. Those of the Hegelings who knew Wate well kept out of his way; he did not stop to ask if he was sweeping friend or foe aside with his sword, merely cut himself a path through the crowd as if it were a thorn thicket.

When Horand saw Ortwin over Wate's shoulder, bloodstained and unconscious, he rode up, his spear resting over his shoulder so that the standard flew around him like a cloak. "Wate," he cried, "who struck down Hilde's son?"

Hartmut heard him in the middle of the fighting; the men of Ortland were pressing in on him to avenge Ortwin's blood. He laughed back, between thrust and parry: "I struck him, Lord Horand!"

Then Horand gave Morung Hilde's standard for safe keeping and went to attack Hartmut. He had difficulty making his way through the Normans, who stood around their leader thick as wheat sheaves in autumn, but he cut himself a narrow path bordered by wounded and dying men, and Hartmut's laughter died away. They were well matched: sparks sprung hissing from their helmets, like sparks flying from a cat's fur stroked the wrong way. Their swords met again and again, till the points of both sword blades were twisted. Hartmut suddenly thrust, and caught Horand on the left shoulder, but Horand bit back his pain and prepared to deal the death blow. At that Lady Gerlind, up on the tower, screamed: a shrill sound like the cry of a sparrowhawk. Ludwig turned and saw his son's desperate need, and threw his own men in between the two enemies. Hard as Horand tried to get back to Hartmut, he was like a swimmer being borne along by the current.

However, in the middle of the bloodstained whirlpool of fighting, Herwig's sharp eyes happened to pick out Lord Ludwig. He thrust aside the men in front of him with his strong arm and shouted, into the thick of battle, "Ludwig! Ludwig! I am Herwig, your mortal enemy! You stole my bride and killed her father. Stand and fight, if you are a man!"

Ludwig heard him and saw the man who called out so loud and clear. "You have no need to threaten me in my own country," he said.

They went for each other like lion and tiger, and their own men came to back them up. Ludwig was an experienced fighter, and he made Herwig stagger and fall on one knee. Then he turned away as if to show that he despised his opponent and thought he had taught him enough of a lesson. The Lord of Zealand leaped up from the ground, his glance searching the castle battlements. A flush of shame rose to Herwig's brown cheeks, and his blood was up now. "Suppose Gudrun saw that old man strike me and escape, when I am so much younger," he thought. "She will despise me when I come to embrace her!"

He mounted his horse and had his blue banner carried before him, telling his men to blow their horns as a signal to attack Ludwig's castle of Karadein. He met with tough resistance from the Normans, who were defending their country as he was his honor.

Ludwig was fighting Frute at the moment when he heard horns blown behind his back. He cast just one glance over his shoulder and saw the blue banner waving outside his castle gateway. "Get back!" he cried. "Get back to the castle!" So the Normans began fighting their way back over the battlefield, as they had fought their way out on to it.

Death reaped his richest harvest where Frute and Wate were fighting. Wate stood there, legs braced apart, swinging his sword with both hands. His battle fury was upon him; Wate was the truest of friends in peace, but in war he was a dreadful enemy. The Normans' feet slipped in pools of blood on the ground all around him; Wate had waited seven years to avenge his overlord's death, and now he was taking his terrible revenge. When Hartmut and his small company of men made toward Ludwig, to cover the old king's retreat to the castle, Wate saw them coming, and flung himself and a thousand of his own men from Sturmen between them and the castle gate.

Lord Hartmut sighed, and said, "I would rather have seen any other gatekeeper there than Wate! God is angry and is making us pay for our sins now. If we were birds we could fly away. If we were moles we could burrow into the ground. But as we are only poor human knights, we cannot escape. Stand firm beside me, then, and make the Hegelings' hot blood flow through the cold rings of their mailshirts!"

Then a battle began around the castle of Karadein, and all the killing before had been nothing to it.

Herwig was still searching for Ludwig; he fought hard and well. He had seen women up on the battlements, but he could not recognize Gudrun today in her veil and chaplet any more than he had recognized her dressed as a poor washerwoman yesterday. Knowing she was near, however, gave him a strength he had never had before. Gritting his teeth, he brought the wily old Ludwig to bay, and finally he saw his moment, swung back his sword and swept it cleanly. He struck Ludwig's head right off, and if Gudrun had seen him brought to his knees earlier, he had made up for it now.

There was loud lamenting up in the castle, a noise of men shouting and of women's cries, high as the scream of gulls.

Hartmut realized that some great misfortune had happened, but he could not turn around; he had to stand and fight all the enemies pressing against him.

Up on the battlements Lady Gerlind was doing as she had promised, getting her servants to throw heavy rocks down on the Hegelings. They killed many men as they came thundering down. And as she had promised, she herself carried as many stones as she could, and hurled them down on the men of Sturmen, cursing wildly.

Wate was like a man drunk with the rage of battle. He stood in the thick cloud of dust raised by the stones falling around him, and it seemed his sword was so sharp it killed with every stroke and never merely wounded. And as he thrust with his sword, he sang songs in a language no one could understand, in time to his strokes.

"None of us will get through that gateway alive so long as Wate stands there outside it," said Hartmut. "I will go and fight him."

He flung himself against an enemy that no one else would have dared seek out on purpose.

"Guard the gate," said Wate to Frute. "I shall soon give Hartmut what he wants!"

Hartmut had never fought better, but everyone could see his death come dancing toward him on the tip of

Wate's sword blade. Up above, Lady Gerlind hung out of the tower window, flinching at every one of Wate's strokes as if it pierced her own heart. Then Ortrun slipped from her side and ran down the stairs to the room in the tower where Gudrun was. She burst in among Gudrun's women and fell at Gudrun's feet, breathless.

"Have mercy! Gudrun, have mercy! Do not let Wate kill Hartmut! Think of your own father's death and have pity on me! I have always been your friend—do not let them kill my brother as well as my father!"

"Indeed you were good to me," said Gudrun, "and I mean to be good to you! But how can I help you now? I am only a girl. If I were a knight, then I would put my shield over Hartmut now, for your sake."

Ortrun shed tears, her young mouth trembling. "Call out to Wate, Gudrun, call out to him!" So Gudrun ran to the window, leaning out over its breastwork, and there she saw Hartmut still fighting, but very nearly at the end of his strength. She shouted as loud as she could, "Wate, Wate! Stop—for my sake, stop!"

But Wate did not hear her; he could not hear anything when the fury of battle was upon him. He raised his sword with both hands, its blade swishing through the air . . . and Gudrun cried out once more, in great terror, because it seemed to her that she herself would bear the guilt for Hartmut's death if she could not save him now. "Uncle! Uncle! It is I, Gudrun!"

Herwig of Zealand heard her, and his heart leaped. Now that Gudrun had begged for mercy for Hartmut, it did not seem a chivalrous thing to watch him die. Herwig threw himself and his shield in front of Hartmut just as the sword blade came whistling down again. His new shield was cut right in two, his new helmet cracked like a hollow nut, the Lord of Zealand staggered at the force of the blow and would have fallen to the ground, covered in blood, if Lord Hartmut had not caught him in his arms.

The King of the Normans looked at Wate and said in a steady voice, "Now do as you like to me. I will not raise my sword against a Hegeling again."

So Hartmut was taken prisoner, along with eighty noble Norman knights, all that were left of his company.

When Hartmut surrendered, those Normans still fighting to reach Karadein knew their castle would not hold out long, but they hoped to sell their lives dearly. The Hegelings were attacking Karadein fiercely now. Men swarmed at the foot of the gateway towers like the shrimps that swarm in the sea at the foot of the cliffs of Normandy. The Normans on the battlements of the castle tower began breaking stones off the breastwork itself to fling down on the Hegelings. The stones fell, rattling, and Wate thundered out orders for his men to hold their shields close together above their heads. Gerlind had mortars, and handmills, and other heavy household implements brought from the kitchen, and threw them down too, killing many brave men. She and her servants poured down boiling water, and when any of her missiles struck home she leaned out over the battlements, listening to the screams and the death cries, and she laughed horribly.

Those of the warriors who had been at the battle on the Wulpensand thought it had been child's play compared to the fighting for Karadein.

But every time Wate heard Gerlind's evil laugh he glanced up, and the look in his eyes boded no good.

He began flinging the Normans out of his path like a wounded bear on its hind legs, striking out with its great paws. Frute kept his back covered all the time. And at last Wate, still fighting, got to the gate. It was made of stout oak planks covered with iron. The Normans shot at him from the gateway towers, an acrid dust swirled up, and stones rattled down from overhead. Spears whistled past his ear, with a sound like silk tearing. But Wate was not fated to die in this battle. He seized an axe from one of the Hegelings and began to batter at the gate; soon all the Normans were trying to kill this one man. Wate flung the axe aside and began shaking the mighty oak planks, cursing the gate which would not budge. He ran at it with his shoulder, snorting, his face distorted, and Gerlind's laugh came from above again.

Wate raised his eyes to her, and her laughter broke off short. The Lord of Sturmen planted his legs wide apart, and raised the sword he had inherited from his ancestors in both hands. It came down with a great crash, and a grinding of iron on iron. Wate began cutting away the hinges one by one, those thick bands of wrought iron which held the castle gate to the great walls of Karadein. And as he struck, his good sword serving him well, Wate started singing a song in that language no other living man knew. His strength seemed to grow the more he needed it. Hinge after hinge broke off, until the door was swaying on the last of them. Then Wate flung his sword aside and began to shake the gate back and forth by its brazen rings, with the strength of twenty-six men.

The Norman women up on the battlements fell to their knees and began praying to God, our Lord and Savior. They said the prayers to be used in the hour of death.

The Normans and the Hegelings were all standing still now, watching Wate. There was a mighty rending sound and a thunderous echo. The gate fell to the ground with a great crash, and Wate, staggering a little, stood back to let Horand pass over it as if it were a wooden bridge, carrying Lady Hilde's banner into the fortress.

The Hegelings burst in after him like the breakers of the sea, leaving many thousand dead behind, but they did not care; what they had done seemed good to them.

They stormed the flight of steps within the defensive outer wall, leading up to the castle itself, and broke the inner gate of the castle down with rams and axes after more hard fighting. And then they had captured both the two proud fortresses of Karadein and Kassiane. They cut down any enemies who still resisted; the Hegelings had paid dearly for the Norman castles, and considered them their own. They filled the tilting yard, they went on and up the stairs like a flood, they made their way into the castle galleries, shouting exultantly, and then the intoxication of their victory took hold of them. They started exchanging their battered swords for new ones, they took new mailshirts to replace the bloodstained ones they were wearing, they seized on cloaks, and veils for their women at home, chains and rings and belts. They opened closets with their swords and flung the lids of chests back against the wall; the Hegelings stopped fighting and loaded themselves up with plunder instead.

Wate stood and watched them, laughing. "Where are the servants to bring us sacks?"

The exhausted Herwig made his way over to Wate, leaning on his sword. He had a bandage around his head, red with blood, as red as the crimson scarf around the Moorish prince's helmet. Herwig was very pale, and his eyes, which were usually as blue as harebells, looked dark.

"Wate, are you going to let the Hegelings take loot like common pirates? This victory has made us heroes—do you want us to be known as thieves?"

He pointed to the men throwing women's robes over their shoulders and clutching golden cups and dishes to their chests. They hesitated, and drew aside.

"Well?" cried Wate, the veins swelling at his temples. "Did the Normans behave differently when they attacked Lady Hilde? We are only taking back our own! And no one gives orders to my men from Sturmen except myself!"

Then Horand signed to Herwig with his eyes to leave Wate alone, and he himself went over to the men and told them, quietly, to remember the oath they had sworn when they were in danger on the sea. The Danish lord promised to give them the full value of the plunder they would have taken, out of his own treasury.

As for Wate himself, he strode on into the very inmost courtyard, where the Normans had withdrawn, still fighting. He was cutting himself a pathway to Gudrun. There was still fierce fighting here, where the best of the Norman knights fought for their lives and their honor, and to protect their queen and princess, defending the doorway to the inner halls.

Gudrun was sitting in the tower with her women. The sound of screams and the clash of swords, the death cries and the noise of falling men which they had heard since sunrise had died away, and now it was night.

As they sat there, their heads covered by their veils, longing now for nothing but an end to all this misery, Ortrun came and knocked on the door. The hostages had barred it on the inside, but she asked them to let her in. Gudrun herself went with the others to pull back the heavy bolts. Ortrun buried her face in her hands, and her hands filled with tears like two white vessels.

"I have come to ask you for help again, Gudrun," she said. "Have pity on us! We have had to leave the hall where we were sitting. Wate is raging outside the door, and we saw the blood of the men we loved come trickling like red snakes under the door toward us. Have mercy on us! There are a thousand swords threatening us!"

Gudrun replied at once, "Come in—come in, with all your women!"

So Ortrun called her ladies, and they all crowded into the room, weeping. Hildburg closed the doors quickly, and they shot all four bolts across, to keep out the sound of the fighting down below.

The room was very full now, as all the women sat or stood or knelt close together. The Norman ladies were praying, many of them rocking back and forth in silent grief like drunken men, many of them biting their handkerchiefs to keep themselves from screaming out loud, many of them staring dry-eyed at the floor as if they could still see those red snakes wriggling toward them—the heart's blood of the men they had loved.

Then Gudrun raised her head and listened. She thought she heard someone sobbing outside the door. She told them all to be quiet, and then they could hear the sound of desperate weeping. Hildburg and Gudrun exchanged glances, and they pushed back the bolts again. They saw a woman lying outside the door face downward, and they knew her by her red hair. The Duchess Heregart raised her head, moaning, to drag herself over to Gudrun on her knees. She spread out her arms, unable to utter a word for shame and grief. She was racked by sobs; she had seen her handsome lover, Gerlind's cupbearer, lying dead, killed by Wate's sword.

Gudrun looked down at her, frowning as she remembered the day Heregart had come riding down to the beach on horseback, with a hawk on her wrist, to watch her mistress wash clothes. But even as her anger rose in her she saw the wet, bloodstained place on Heregart's breast where she had cradled her dying lover's head. Gudrun thought of Herwig, and said quietly, "Take your place at my left hand, Heregart." After that they said no more.

But as they sat in silence they heard the noise of fighting coming closer and closer, as if the bloody tide of death were lapping up to them.

Then a hand took the door latch and shook it; they all drew together in fear as fists beat against the wood. But Gudrun could hear how weak the sound was. Little Hildburg stood up, but Gudrun put out a hand to hold her back. They went on listening, rooted to the spot, and the fists drummed on the door yet again.

"Gudrun," said Hildburg, her slender body held very upright, "as you are now, so Our Lord will be to you on the day you die."

And Gudrun dropped her hand. When Hildburg had drawn back the bolts again, Gerlind fell on her knees in the doorway. The change in her was dreadful to see. Locks of gray and white hair hung down over her hollow cheeks, her eyes shot wildly back and forth, her chin was trembling like the chin of a child about to burst into tears. The rags of her rich robes hung around her. She was covered with mortar and dust from the stones she had carried, and she reached her scratched hands out to Gudrun.

"Mercy!" she gasped. "Save me from Wate! He is hunting me to my death—he is coming after me!" And she crawled to Gudrun on her knees. "I will serve you, I will nurse Herwig's children for you, but do not let me fall into that murdering devil's hands!"

There was a deep frown between Gudrun's brows. "Were you ever so kind to me, Lady Gerlind, that you should come expecting mercy from me now?"

Gerlind groaned aloud, and there was mortal terror in her face; it was a horrible sight. Her hand pointed to the arched window, and when they looked out they could see Wate starting up the stairway to the tower where Gudrun was.

One of Gerlind's own men stood on every step of that

stairway, and little as they had loved Lady Gerlind, Wate had to fight every one of them before he could reach the next step. But the grim executioner was climbing on and on. Before he struck down each Norman with his dreadful sword, its central groove running with blood, he said to him, "Bring me Gerlind's head, and you shall live." But every one of them preferred to die fighting.

Hildburg could not bear to see Gerlind's frantic terror any longer. Quietly, she took her hand and led her into the very midst of Gudrun's ladies. No one spoke a word.

There had been no time to lose. Outside, Wate had killed the last of the guards and fought his way right to the top step. They heard his iron tread upon the floor, they stood close together as his heavy hand took hold of the door latch, and they flinched when his voice called, "Whoever it is in there, come out!"

They all held their breath.

They heard him shaking at the latch, and the hinges of the doors groaned. Their eyes were all on the wooden planks, no one dared move or scream; it was like a nightmare when you cannot cry out . . .

One mighty heave, and the doors were pulled outward, the wooden bolts cracked and splintered, and then the doors flew back against the wall. There stood Wate.

The women screamed at once with a single shrill cry. Wate was a dreadful sight. His shield and his great helmet had both been cut in two; he carried no weapon but his sword, which was notched and toothed like a saw. Blood dripped from his clothes onto the floor, and ran from his own head wound into his eyebrows and his long beard, dark streaks of red among its white hairs. His eyeballs were fiery red, and they had an evil gleam in them. He was grinding his teeth as they say a man does when bloodlust overcomes him.

"Where is Gerlind?" he growled. "Where is that she-devil Gerlind?"

Gudrun plucked up all her courage. She stepped forward, smiling, bowed courteously and said in a loud voice, as if to awaken him, and as cheerfully as she could, "You are very welcome, Wate! Glad as I am to see you, I should be even happier if you had not left so much suffering behind you as you came."

Wate passed his hand over his forehead, like a man waking from a dream. Suddenly he seemed so tired that he leaned against the wall. "Forgive me, noble lady! Are you Hilde's daughter? And who are these standing around you?"

"These are the poor girls who came over the sea with me, Uncle Wate!"

"Forgive me, noble lady, but are there no Norman women here?"

Gudrun said, quickly and firmly, "Yes, Lord Wate. Here is Ortrun, with her ladies, and she has been like a sister to me all this time!"

Then Wate said, the evil light in his eyes again, "But is there no other Norman woman here? A woman who made you wash clothes on the icy beach?"

Gudrun bowed her head to her breast, but she spoke out, soft and clear. "There is no one here on whom I wish to avenge myself, Uncle Wate!"

Wate came up to her, his face so terrible that Gudrun put out her hands to keep him off. "If you do not point her out to me, niece, the innocent will suffer for it!"

Striding forward, he pushed aside the women with both his arms until he saw Lady Gerlind's gray head among all the younger heads, both fair and dark. He seized her and dragged her out, flinging her to the floor at Gudrun's feet. "Tell me now, Lady Gerlind," he said, his whole body shaking with rage, "shall my lady and my queen wash any more dirty clothes for you?"

Then he swooped down like a vulture taking its prey, and grasped her by the hair. Winding Gerlind's gray locks around his wrist, he dragged her to the doorway. Once outside he kicked the doors shut again, so that Gudrun would not see what was to happen now.

They heard a whirring sound, and a cry that chilled the blood, the sound of a blow and the sound of a fall—and then utter silence.

There was not one of them who had not seemed to feel the sword on her own neck.

Wate came in again, staggering against the doorpost.

"I have one more woman to find today," he said. "I want Heregart, the mistress of Lady Gerlind's cupbearer!"

At that, Hildburg fell on her knees to him, and so did the others. Gudrun begged him to be merciful and end the bloodshed now.

"I cannot be merciful," said Wate. "I am Lady Hilde's chamberlain, it is my duty to keep order among her women!"

When he had said that, Heregart stepped out, her red head held proudly high. She stood in front of Wate, and she made no sound as she fell, but she dragged herself back to Gudrun, looking at her, and she died silently at Gudrun's left hand, where her place had been in her life.

After he struck that blow, Wate dropped his sword with a great clang and blew his horn, to bring the fighting in the castle to an end.

The great horn itself fell from his hands; Lord Wate staggered and fell on the floor where he was. He slept for three nights and three days, and no one could wake him, or lift him and carry him to a bed. So they left him alone, and when he woke he was the man they knew, a faithful friend but a terrible enemy.

When the Hegelings heard Wate's horn, they threw their shields and swords aside and ran to the castle wells to wash the taste of blood from their lips. They were all laughing like boys because the Hegelings themselves looked as dark-skinned as the Moors, with the marks of their iron helmets on their faces, while the Moors were white from the dust and mortar of the falling stones.

When Herwig had washed, and his hair and handsome face were their own brown color again, he put on clean clothes and went up to find Gudrun. Dark as it was outside, she knew him by his footsteps and the beating of her own heart, and she laughed, tremulously.

Herwig came up to her there in the hall and spread out his arms. Seven years sank away, as if they had never been; the dead and living around them seemed to melt away too, suffering and guilt seemed to melt away, all the bitterness between their first kiss and this one might never have been at all.

They clung so close together that neither of them saw Ortwin stride into the hall. Ortrun laid her finger on her lips to warn him to keep silent, and Ortwin found himself looking at a girl with new eyes for the first time. Ortrun blushed, seeing him gaze so long. It seemed magical to her to see Gudrun's golden eyes and smile, but in a man's face. Lord Horand stood quietly in the doorway and rejoiced to see the first threads of love spun between them.

It was Hildburg who interrupted the happy lovers; she had seen Lord Morung and she flew to her father's arms with a cry of joy. There were cries of welcome, and many questions and answers and much rejoicing. Quietly, Frute had the blood washed from the stairs and walls and the dead men carried out of the castle, while the women fell into the Hegelings' arms.

Frute had the corpses put into ships, and when the whole sad cargo was aboard, he ordered the anchors to be raised. The strong ships went out into the night, enemy lying by enemy and companion by good companion. The stormy wind chased clouds over the sky, and old Frute watched for a long time as the fleet carried eight thousand silent warriors away to that strange coast where we shall all land, and yet which none of us knows.

The Hegelings carried Lady Hilde's standard all through the land of Normandy. Many of them went in hopes of destroying the strong castles and plundering the rich countryside, but though he gave few of his good reasons for it, Frute persuaded them to leave the land alone. He made Lord Irold Protector of Normandy, to stay behind with a thousand of the best men, and then Frute set about preparing for the journey home.

The Hegelings took Hartmut down to their ships. He had been imprisoned in conditions worthy of a knight, and his many wounds were healed; Hildburg had gone to nurse him herself, in secret. But he was pale and sad.

"Noble lords" he said very quietly, "I could wish you would leave me in my father's land. I would give you all I own as a token of peace."

"We'd rather have you yourself!" laughed Wate. "And

if my nephew Ortwin would listen to me, I'd make sure your bonds need not trouble you any longer!"

"What would be the use of killing him?" asked Ortwin, indignantly. "I intend to bring my noble hostages to my mother honorably!" And once they had put out to sea he took off Hartmut's fetters himself.

Gudrun was standing on deck at Herwig's side, her hands in his. He saw with surprise, and with uneasiness in his heart, that her golden eyes were clouded and her lovely lips trembled.

"My dearest," he said, "surely you are glad to be going home?"

"Oh, yes!" she said, smiling through her tears. "But I was thinking of the years I spent in this country, all those years washing clothes on the shore we are passing now. There is no king on earth powerful enough or God in heaven great enough to give them back to me!"

As she was speaking Horand came up to her. "Lady Gudrun," he asked, "who is that woman standing on the shore, smiling and waving both her hands to you?"

Then the princess recognized the woman, who had waded barefoot as far as she could out into the sea. Her gray hair was blowing in the wind, her red shawl fluttered as she held herself upright against the incoming waves, which washed right up to her heavy wooden clogs where they stood on the pebbles. It was the washerwoman who had taught Gudrun to wash clothes, smiling all over her good-natured face because now Gudrun could go home again.

As for Gudrun, she flushed a deep red. "Oh Horand," she stammered, "you brought me up so well, and now you find me doing wrong! I was complaining of my own troubles and forgetting someone who was so good to me! Please, get them to put out a boat and row me to the shore. I will give her lands and castles for the help she gave us in our wretchedness!"

Horand smiled at Gudrun and said he thought the washerwoman would rather have a farm and fields of good Norman earth than any of Hartmut's castles. So Gudrun gave the old woman good fertile land near Karadein, and a great herd of the heavy, spotted Norman cattle for herself and her six fair-headed sons. They became a strong and notable family, and they adopted a wooden clog as their coat of arms and bore it proudly ever afterward.

Spring had come to the coasts along which the ships were sailing, and the thrushes were singing. The sea itself was smooth as green meadows. The Hegelings had decked their masts with young green leaves, and the men sang during the ships' watches. As Gudrun lay awake, unable to sleep for joy, she heard the old sea songs once more and smiled in the dark. One day she asked Horand to sing, saying she had been longing for his songs, as if they were all she needed now to set the seal on her happiness.

She was amazed to hear of his oath, and coaxed him to sing for a long time, saying it was all over now, and he had kept his word. But Horand shook his head, saying Hilde and Gudrun had not kissed each other yet. So the sweetest songs they heard on the ships were the old sea songs, echoing and familiar as the sea itself, and all the other music they had was the thin piping of the little wooden flutes that the Moorish warriors blew at night as they crouched on the decks of their tall ships, shivering, wrapped in their white cloaks.

Gudrun remembered the journey to Normandy, when she had been carried away, and she wept as she heard the Norman hostages weeping secretly into their pillows now. She could not shut her ears to them; she got up and went barefoot to Ortrun's bed. She kissed Ortrun and comforted her, and gave her and her ladies all the precious things she could lay hands upon, making them solemn promises, until at last they plucked up courage again.

One morning a cry rang out from the masthead, echoing like a song. "Land ahead! Our own land ahead!"

Flushed, newly roused from sleep, the men ran on deck, unwilling to believe any eyes but their own. Gudrun saw the steep, rugged cliffs of the land of the Hegelings, overlaid by the golden light of dawn, as she had seen them in her dreams. She fell into Hildburg's arms. Hildburg was laughing and crying, like Gudrun herself.

Herwig sent two messengers on ahead in a fast boat,

with the very best of the Arab horses. Once on land they abandoned the boat and mounted, and their noble horses began to race on, keeping step with one another. They rode all that day and the whole night. The sentries of Matalane saw the two riders far away, spurring their horses on to a last effort, and they smiled broadly; everyone knows that bearers of bad news do not come in such a hurry.

The two messengers were waving and shouting as they rode in, and the sentries blew their horns with all their might. Lady Hilde herself ran down, and by the time the Zealanders had dismounted from their trembling horses she was at the gate. She wore deep mourning, as she had done ever since the battle on the Wulpensand.

"Is my daughter alive? Is Lord Ortwin alive?" she asked breathlessly.

"All is well! It could not have been better! Lord Herwig is bringing Lady Gudrun to you, and Wate has taken the Norman king and princess and is bringing them as prisoners!"

Then Lady Hilde took one lone, shuddering breath, and silently she loosed the black veil from her hair. She gave the messengers such rewards as even the bringers of good news never got before. They were simple squires when they knelt before her, but when they rose to their feet they were lords of rich castles.

"But now, lady, make haste to prepare for so many

guests!" said one of the messengers. Lady Hilde only smiled. If she had spent seven years after the battle on the Wulpensand preparing for her expedition to set out, she had spent every day since the men left preparing for their return.

The messengers were amazed to see rows and rows of tables already standing under the green beech trees, with long benches which were quickly covered with cushions and bright hangings woven by Hilde and her ladies. A long line of fires was lit, and whole oxen and boars began to turn on the shining spits. Pavilions were raised over poles set in the ground ready for them, furs were heaped up to make couches—couches as soft as any mother could make for her child.

One bright, sunny morning the ships which had set out in winter put in to land. The birds were singing for joy in the trees, the grass was full of flowers in full bloom, there was a warm scent on the wind, and the apple trees bore blossoms like snow.

Lady Hilde rode down to the shore, wearing royal robes with gleaming stones worked into the silk. Her cheeks were red and white as roses under her snowy hair. She rode slowly; she was secretly afraid she might not recognize her dear child Gudrun after these seven long years, and she had lain awake all night thinking of nothing else.

There were more than a hundred women on board the

ships, and the warriors began to lead them over a narrow gangplank which had to be laid from the ships to land, because the breakers were rough and the sea was full of rocks near the coast of the Hegelings' land. Wate helped some of the women to land first, not being quite sure in his own mind how safe the gangplank was, and then he went back for Gudrun. She was in a great hurry to get to shore, having seen her mother's white hair on the beach, and so it happened that she slipped on the swaying gangplank. At that Lady Hilde, pierced to the heart, cried out, "Gudrun, take care!" and ran toward the ships.

It was only when Wate placed Gudrun safely in her arms that Lady Hilde really came to her senses. Then she smiled to think she had been afraid all night that a mother's heart could ever forget her child.

When Gudrun let her mother go at last, Ortwin took Lady Hilde in his own arms. The queen exchanged kisses with Herwig and Wate too, with Frute of Denmark, and Morung, and the Prince of the Moors. Last of all, Lord Horand came forward and took her kiss upon his aching lips.

"Now you must kiss Hildburg too, Mother," said Gudrun. "She was always loyal to me!"

Tenderly, Lady Hilde kissed the small face under the mass of black hair.

Then Gudrun took Ortrun's hand and led her to Lady

Hilde. "And you must kiss her too, Mother, for my sake."

"Who is this girl?" asked Hilde, frowning. "I do not kiss anyone I do not know."

"Dearest Mother," said Gudrun, "this is Ortrun of Normandy, and she was my friend all the time!"

"If she was your friend in Normandy," said Lady Hilde, "then I will be her friend in the land of the Hegelings!" And she bent and kissed Ortrun's trembling mouth.

"I shall not forget your kindness, Sister!" Ortwin whispered into Gudrun's ear.

The Hegelings went up to Matalane castle, where Lady Hilde entertained them royally. They rested for five days; wherever you went you might have stumbled over a man fast asleep in the green grass, with a pillow under his head, with the bees humming around him and the scent of wild thyme in the air, warm in the sun.

On the sixth day Gudrun took Hildburg aside. "Were you so unused to happiness in Normandy that you cannot enjoy it again now you are home?"

"I am not like you," said Hildburg, with a touch of bitterness. "I cannot be happy while others are sad."

"Why, when we have given so many gifts in our gratitude, is there still anyone discontented at Matalane?" asked Gudrun, though she knew what Hildburg meant well enough.

"You have forgotten Lord Hartmut," said Hildburg, very quietly, playing with the end of her belt. "His fate has not been decided yet, and I hear him sighing and lamenting at night."

"Then we will not forget him any longer," Gudrun promised. "Come with me, and call Ortrun too!"

She led both the girls to Hilde, who was sitting in her hall.

"Dearest Mother," said Gudrun, "for the sake of your own good name do not repay bad with worse!"

"If any such thing has happened, it is not with my knowledge or my wish," said Lady Hilde, "and may God pardon me for it!"

Then Ortrun fell on her knees. "My brother and all our kindred have been lying in prison ever since they came to Matalane."

Gudrun laid her hand on Ortrun's bright hair and, with tears in her own eyes, she said. "It would do you nothing but honor, Mother, if you showed mercy now and set Hartmut free to wear his crown."

But Hildburg's tears were the hottest of all, though she could only clasp her hands in front of her trembling lips and gaze at Lady Hilde mutely.

Lady Hilde smiled, and raised the three girls from their knees. "Spare your beautiful eyes, do not shed any more tears! If you can get Hartmut to swear he will not try to escape in secret, he shall go free and be my guest at this court, with all his men."

Hartmut willingly promised not to escape, and his

chains were taken off. Gudrun ordered baths and rich robes to be prepared for the Normans, so that they could come to court as the noble knights they were. A great banquet was made ready for that evening, and the Hegelings began to wake from their sleep, and stretch, as if the day of judgment had come.

When Hartmut joined the other lords, dressed like a great prince, Hildburg was not the only lady to think him worth a melting glance. The Hegelings welcomed him heartily, and there was such goodwill that even Wate drank to Hartmut's health.

And so it seemed that all hearts were easy at last. There was jousting and feasting every day; Matalane had never known a merrier time. Yet Lord Herwig was restless and distracted; he could not settle to anything, and he had horses and weapons made ready in secret.

Lady Hilde saw that he was uneasy, and when she gently asked him why, Herwig said frankly that he was afraid of losing Gudrun, as he had done once already, and he would not feel certain of his good fortune until she was married to him and wore the crown of Zealand. So, he said, with Lady Hilde's permission he would like to set off with his bride for his own home the next day.

Hilde asked him a favor: to let Gudrun be crowned and married to him at Matalane, with all her family there, and Herwig agreed with all his heart, so long as it might be soon.

Lady Hilde began preparing a wedding for her child which would be fit for the daughter of a queen of thirty kingdoms. She would not let any of the lords ride away from court yet, not even the Prince of the Moors—and as for him, he was glad enough to stay, because the count's daughter was there, the girl with the freckles and merry little nose who had woken Gudrun on the day the Hegelings came to set her free. Her bright eyes had dwelt on the Prince of the Moors and his brown face between his golden earrings, and they had fallen deeply in love, conversing by means of sighs and glances and a mixture of words from their two languages.

Lady Hilde opened wide her chambers, and they could all see how hard she and her women had worked over the long years. There were festive robes for any who wanted them, and whatever any of the Hegelings or Moors or Normans asked, Lady Hilde gave them double the amount. The heroes exchanged gifts freely themselves. Wate gave his friends anything they wanted, and Horand was so generous it looked as though he were determined to end his days penniless.

Lord Ortwin gave new weapons and clothes to five hundred noble squires who were about to be made knights, and Frute gave them horses of the best Danish breed, and rich saddlecloths.

Lord Hartmut was the only one who stood aside while all this giving and receiving of gifts went on, his thin cheeks turning red and white with shame as he stared at his empty hands.

Lady Hilde saw what troubled him, and when he went back to his own room that evening he found ten chests there full of royal treasures. He laughed aloud for joy, understanding that Hilde had not wanted to deprive him of the greatest of all pleasures: the sight of happy faces as friends received his gifts. Next morning there was not a bracelet left in those chests: Hartmut had given everything away.

Each of the lords had his own task as in the old days. Wate and Irold were the queen's chamberlains, Frute was her steward, Horand was her cupbearer. Now Gudrun and Herwig had made a plan: Gudrun had noticed how rosily Ortrun of Normandy blushed whenever Ortwin came near her, and how pale she turned when he went away, so she took her brother by the hand and led him into her own chamber. "As your sister," said she, "let me give you some good advice; if you feel the way that I think you do, we could both be married on the same day!"

Ortwin hung his head, and told her what had been troubling him for days: there was the shadow of death and vengeance standing between him and his beloved Ortrun, he said, and so thought she could never be his. All the time he held her in his arms she would be grieving for the dead.

"She will soon stop grieving if you go about it the right way," laughed Gudrun. "I think you should marry, and I think she is the girl for you—I tell you so as truly as she was true to me! She will never make you unhappy."

Ortwin gazed at her, wide-eyed, then he left her standing there and ran straight out of her chamber. The door swung open behind him, and he heard Gudrun's clear laughter follow him.

The Hegelings were sitting feasting, but Ortwin was not there. They had nearly finished their meal, and were eating the sweet cakes, when the King of Ortland came in, leading Ortrun by the hand, her face pinker than summer roses.

"So you are to be my dear daughter!" said Lady Hilde. "And we will make up all the old quarrels between our countries!"

Frute leaned over to Gudrun, saying with his gentle smile, "Now you only have one of your plans left to carry out, lady!"

"Why—do you know about that too, Lord Frute?" said Gudrun in surprise.

And that night, when all the other women were asleep, Gudrun whispered, "Hildburg?" She heard her friend tossing and turning restlessly. Hildburg, who had been crying, lay still and held her breath. "Do not cry," said Gudrun softly. "Come here to me." In the dim glow of the nightlight, Hildburg came and sat at the foot of

Gudrun's bed. Gudrun sat up and wound Hildburg's hair around her fingers. "My dearest friend," she whispered, without looking up, "I am going to reward you for your constancy to me. You shall wear the crown of Normandy!"

Hildburg was horrified. "Are you going to rob Lord Hartmut of his inheritance and give me that for a reward? That would be shameful! I will never agree to it!"

"Ah, but you shall wear the crown of Normandy as his queen!"

Hildburg stood up, white as death. "Would you force a man who never loved me to marry me, Gudrun? If he and I were to spend our lives together, I should often suffer for it!"

"Hartmut is not the same man he was when Gerlind was alive to lead him astray," Gudrun whispered. "And he knows how much you have done for him. It seems to me he looks at you in a different way now."

"Is that true, Gudrun?" stammered little Hildburg. "Dear God, do you think it might be true?" It was the first time Hildburg had ever confided her love to anyone else, though it had brought her such grief for so long.

In the morning Gudrun summoned Hartmut, and spoke to him. There was no one else there but the wise old counselor Frute.

"Will you trust me, Lord Hartmut?" she asked, meeting his gaze. His eyes were grave.

"I never knew you be anything but open and straightforward, Lady Gudrun."

"Then I think you should marry now, Lord Hartmut, and marry the wife I choose for you. You shall have back your freedom and the crown of Normandy as her dowry!"

Lord Hartmut took three steps backward, shaking his head. "Lady Gudrun, I would rather lose my land and my life than marry anyone on such conditions. My friends would all despise me bitterly for getting back my castles in that way!"

"Hartmut!" said Gudrun softly. "Yesterday your sister Ortrun was betrothed to my young brother, and now, at last, there will be peace between us. And if you marry Hildburg, no one will ever have won a more willing heart. She has loved you secretly a very long time."

Lord Hartmut looked into Gudrun's face, and thought he had never seen such a sweet, piercing look in it as now, when she was telling him to marry Hildburg. He turned away his head in pain, gnawing his lip, at a loss for words.

And as he turned his face away from Gudrun, he suddenly seemed to see the hall window of Matalane before him; there had been a girl standing there when he rode to the castle to see Gudrun for the first time. He saw the pretty girl look at him, unable to stop the blood rising suddenly in her small face, crowned by its black hair. He saw Hildburg secretly nursing his wounds, he remembered that she had knelt to beg for his life, and he was touched, as he had often been recently when he thought of her. Without raising his eyes from the floor, Hartmut of Normandy said, "I will do as you wish."

But when he looked up to see Gudrun reaching out both hands to him with a happy laugh, he thought once again that the wandering minstrels had been right when they sang that the gold of her eyes was more precious than all the crowns on earth.

Lord Wate of Sturmen said the Normans must go through the old ceremony of expiation before the wedding: it was a holy custom, and he thought it would mean bad luck for the people if they did not observe it. So a day was fixed, and when it came the Hegelings and Normans stood in the hall, drawn up to the right and left of Lady Hilde's seat. Trumpets sounded, and Lord Hartmut of Normandy came in, holding his sister's hand, and went up to the queen's seat. Hartmut and Ortrun both fell on their knees and spoke together, speaking from the heart as they recited the ancient words asking forgiveness for the blood that had been shed, and the forgetting of past sins. Wate and Horand stood above them with drawn swords all the time, as if they were to be executed if Hilde refused to forgive them. When she embraced the kneeling pair, they lowered their swords, wiping them as if they were wiping blood off the blades.

Lord Wate gave Hartmut his strong right hand, saying, "Now my lady has kissed you, this hand is at your service whenever you need it. And you, if anyone, should know the kind of blows it can strike!"

Then all the noble knights were summoned to the betrothal ceremony. The brides were led in: there were three of them, because the future Queen of the Moors was among them. Herwig and Gudrun, who had exchanged rings long ago, sat and watched while the others were betrothed. The knights formed a circle round the brides, spear close by spear, their faces full of laughter under their warlike helmets. The custom was for the bridegroom to break into the circle and win his bride.

The Prince of the Moors was the first to break in. He put a ring with a black stone of a kind never seen in the Hegelings' land before on his bride's hand, and she seemed to understand him very well, because she answered fluently, though shyly, in the same language. It was easy to see that women will take to new ways more readily than men when they fall in love, since when it was time for the Prince of the Moors to kiss his betrothed wife, he did not know what to do, as the people of his country do not kiss. All the knights laughed when the count's daughter stood on tiptoe to kiss her bridegroom with all her heart.

Then Hartmut came up and parted the shields. He strode firmly up to Hildburg, who swayed on her feet as if she felt dizzy, and spoke to her gently as he placed Gerlind's ring on her finger.

Ortwin was last: the Hegeling knights, laughing, took much longer to let him through to win his bride. He grew quite angry, his eyes flashing, by the time he managed to pluck Ortrun out through the wall of shields, saying he had had to fight quite enough to win her already!

After that they celebrated the weddings. King Ortwin made many good men knights, and there was a tournament so magnificent that it would certainly provide wandering minstrels with subjects for new songs for years to come.

The feasting and rejoicing went on for five days.

On the sixth day Lady Hilde asked the musicians to stop playing. She said, "This is the moment I have waited for so long. Now, after seven years, Lord Horand will sing again, for the first time."

Then the other minstrels drew back as foxes draw back from a lion. Horand's harp was brought to him, and he slowly took off its soft leather wrappings, with fingers unused to the feel of it.

He struck a chord, and a shudder went through everyone there. His head bent, Horand began to play as if he were listening to whatever the strings had to tell him. And he sang the song the Saracen woman taught him, which he had sung only once in his life before, when he was sitting with Lady Hilde in the hall of Ballygan in Ireland, on a warm night much like this:

> Love comes only once, and life is nothing but a cold grave to the man who never knows it.
> Love comes only once, and its sweetness is bitter, but though it may be bitter as gall, that bitterness is sweeter than any sweetness.
> Love comes only once, and I die a thousand deaths daily. But seeing you, I turn my face to the East, and I praise God, the great, the one true God, who lets me die for love of you and rise again, and burn for love of you once more.

The Prince of the Moors came and bent his knee to Horand, his golden armor clashing. "My mother," he said, "told me to kneel like this if ever I met a Western man who could sing that song." Lord Horand looked long into his proud face, and then embraced him and kissed his brow.

And the Prince of the Moors rose and went out into the night, with his little freckled bride following him, obeying his sign to her, just as Moorish women follow their husbands.

Lord Horand sang again, and the words dropped from his lips like wild honey. His tune was sweet and strange and wild; no one there had ever heard it before, and no one who heard it now could ever forget it again. Many of those in the hall bowed their faces in their hands, feeling old wounds begin to bleed, and others stood staring with hard and hungry eyes at faces turned away from them, and others again smiled in astonishment, because they had never looked the power of love in the face before.

As Horand played, Herwig and Gudrun, who were sitting at different places in the hall, rose at the same time. Their outstretched hands met, and they went out, hand in hand, into the night. The stars in their cold and lonely height seemed to tremble at the sight of such happiness.

Then Ortwin and Ortrun went out of the hall too, exchanging more kisses than there were stars in the sky.

And Hartmut's head was low on his breast. Hildburg laid her hand gently on his arm, and he sat up and looked at her, and led her out of the hall. Under the stars he held her tender body close to his, as a freezing man will clutch a blanket to him in the night.

And the song grew and grew, filling the room, pushing back the walls of the hall and letting in the whole starry sky.

None of the few still sitting in the hall could bear it. At last, only Hilde was left there beside the singer.

She sat there, living her life over again as she looked back, and perhaps there is nothing more bitter than to stand at the crossroads once again, and see that you chose to go the wrong way.

So the night passed by, and the stars went out.

Lord Horand looked around him; the flickering torches cast huge shadows on the walls and he was alone with the shadows.

Now we have only to tell of the great leavetaking on the tenth day, when there were many words and gifts of love, many kisses and tears. They all rode down to the ships in great troops.

The Prince of the Moors was taking his queen home, far over the sea to Alzabé. Lord Wate was on his way back to his land of Sturmen. Ortwin and fair Ortrun went to their kingdom of Ortland. Lord Morung went home to his kingdom of Frisia, far away.

But when Hartmut was to leave with his queen, it seemed as if Gudrun could not bear to let Hildburg go. She blessed her a thousand times for her loyal friendship, and kissed Hildburg's little brown face, gazing at it for a long time and knowing she was not likely to see it again.

Horand boarded the same ship as Hartmut and Hildburg, to take Irold news of the peace they had made and tell him Hartmut was to be king again. When Gudrun kissed Horand goodbye she saw how many gray hairs autumn had woven into his hair, and she was sorry. She flung her arms around him and kissed the mouth to which the gift of song had been given.

Last of all, Herwig and Gudrun left Matalane, which was very quiet now. Hilde wept so much that Herwig promised, with all his heart, to send her good messengers three times a year bringing news of Gudrun.

Then they rode down to the sea along a path which looked as if it were covered with some strange writing, their companions had left so many horses' hoofprints behind them.

Gudrun turned around again and again as she rode away, waving to her mother, while Herwig's brown hand held her horse's reins. She looked up at the battlements of Matalane for a long time, seeing Lady Hilde's white handkerchief wave back.

And this is the end of the story of Gudrun.

AFTERWORD

We know the story of *Gudrun*, in the first place, from a long poem which was written in Middle High German, probably by an Austrian poet in the middle of the thirteenth century. It has survived only because Emperor Maximilian I liked to think of himself as the last representative of medieval chivalry, and had a collection of medieval poems, including *Gudrun*, made in the early years of the sixteenth century.

Like various other stories popular in the Middle Ages, such as those of King Arthur and the knights of the Round Table, *Gudrun* is a heroic romance where a medieval code of Christian chivalry has transformed older, sometimes pre-Christian, legends. In this version by Alma Johanna Koenig, as in the original poem, the figure of fierce old Wate, for instance, often comes closer to being a pagan berserk warrior than the ideal of a perfect Christian knight.

The poem of *Gudrun* is thought of as a companion piece to the more famous *Nibelungenlied*, which dates from the same period and is much better known to English-speaking people, no doubt partly because Richard Wagner based his cycle of operas, *The Ring of the Nibelung*, on the same material as the subject of that poem. It has been said that *Gudrun* is to the *Nibelungenlied* as Homer's *Odyssey* is to the *Iliad*, and though it would be risky to take the comparison too far, there is something in it. *Gudrun*, like the *Odyssey*, is full of ships and sea and voyages. The "thirty countries" around the mouth of the river Scheldt and the North Sea coasts of the Netherlands, Germany and Denmark, which owe allegiance to Gudrun's father Hettel, would all be very small by modern standards, like Odysseus's island kingdom of Ithaca. The psychology of the characters, and the details of their background, are just as important as the big scenes of battle and bloodshed. One of the most striking features of the whole story is the active importance of the women characters, culminating in the long battle of wills between the villainous Gerlind, Queen of Normandy, and her proud but patient hostage Gudrun.

In the 1920s, about eight hundred years after the poem was first written down in its surviving form, another

Austrian writer was attracted to the story and wrote this version of it in modern German prose. Alma Johanna Koenig, who was already known as a poet and novelist, took some ideas from another medieval poem about the wooing of Gudrun's mother Hilde by the singer Horand, picked up hints from *Gudrun* itself and expanded them, and while keeping quite close to the original poem she made the story her own.

Alma Johanna Koenig was born in Prague in 1887, but the year after her birth her family moved to Vienna. Her first poems appeared in 1918. This version of *Gudrun*, which became a classic of German literature for young people, was published in 1928. In 1942 Alma Johanna Koenig, as a Jewess, was deported from Vienna to the concentration camp of Minsk. Unlike Gudrun, she was to have no happy ending; nothing more was ever heard of her.

ANTHEA BELL